Can Capitalism Survive?

*the text of this book is printed
on 100% recycled paper*

Can Capitalism Survive?

Joseph A. Schumpeter

HARPER COLOPHON BOOKS
Harper & Row, Publishers
New York, Hagerstown, San Francisco, London

This book was originally published as Part II of *Capitalism, Socialism and Democracy.*

CAN CAPITALISM SURVIVE? Copyright 1942, 1947 by Joseph A. Schumpeter. Copyright 1950 by Harper & Row, Publishers, Inc. Introduction copyright © 1978 by Robert Lekachman. All rights reserved. Printed in the United States of America. No part of this book may be used or reproduced in any manner whatsoever without written permission except in the case of brief quotations embodied in critical articles and reviews. For information address Harper & Row, Publishers, Inc., 10 East 53d Street, New York, N.Y. 10022. Published simultaneously in Canada by Fitzhenry & Whiteside Limited, Toronto.

First HARPER COLOPHON edition published 1978

ISBN: 0-06-090595-6

78 79 80 81 82 10 9 8 7 6 5 4 3 2 1

CONTENTS

INTRODUCTION

I F Nobel prizes were awarded posthumously, Joseph Alois Schumpeter, a transplanted Middle European who was born in Triesch, Moravia, and who devoted the last eighteen years of his life to teaching at Harvard, would surely merit the honor, preferably with an oak leaf cluster. More than a generation after his death in 1950, he is universally esteemed as a great economist even by those legions of specialists who have never read a word he wrote. That minority among economists who retain an appropriate respect for the history of their subject still value his first major work, the 1912 *The Theory of Economic Development*. This brilliant theoretical sketch of capitalist behavior sounded the major theme of its author's lifework, a fascination with economic and social systems. As an economist, Schumpeter no doubt judged as his magnum opus his massive two-volume treatise *Business Cycles*. Published in 1939, it combined historical illustration, speculative analysis, and statistical evidence, all in the service of comprehending the dynamics of cyclical fluctuations.

A polymath and a linguist, Schumpeter seldom neglected the connections between economic phenomena and the cultural and historical context in which they were embedded. His *History of Economic Analysis,* prepared for publication after his death by his widow, herself an economist, carefully refrained from exaggerating the significance of the economic strand in human history. Incomplete though it was, the *History* is a panoramic treatment of the evolution of social thought, to be placed on the same shelf as John Herman Randall's *The Making of the Modern Mind*. Schumpeter was an unashamed big thinker in a period when most of his colleagues were thinking smaller and smaller thoughts about less and less significant issues.

As a person, Schumpeter was the stuff of legend. He was an enormously popular teacher, at his best with small seminar groups, but apparently incapable of delivering a dull lecture even to masses of auditors. With students and colleagues his relations were warm and his argumentative techniques courtly rather than abrasive. In a moment of impatience with the stately manners of the Austrian Empire, a radical colleague termed him "a feudal remnant." His career in fact resembled neither that of an aristocrat nor a sheltered academic. He served briefly after the First World War as Austrian Minister of Finance, subsequently practiced law in Cairo, and then assumed the presidency of an Austrian bank. Its failure was one of a series that culminated in the collapse of the Creditanstalt and the precipitation of the Great Depression.

Schumpeter was a full-blooded celebrant of life. As the possibly apocryphal tale goes, he recalled in his sixties that as a young man he had aspired to be the finest horseman, lover of beautiful women, and economist of his time.

According to one version of the story, he confessed that he had never
learned to ride a horse. Oral tradition offers as an alternative punch line his
comment that he had achieved two of his youthful objectives. What counts
of course is not the literal truth of such illustrative anecdotes but their
plausible attachment to a given individual.

Somewhat belatedly the American Economic Association honored him
with its presidency. Lesser men (no woman has ever received this professional accolade) were not compelled to wait until their late sixties to be so
distinguished. Large-scale theory is an awkward phenomenon for economists. Like Veblen and for somewhat similar reasons, Schumpeter founded
no school. The world abounds in Friedmanites and anti-Friedmanites, Keynesians, neo-Keynesians, and anti-Keynesians, and almost as many versions
of Marx as there are Marxists to propound them.

Why some prophets do collect disciples and others don't is an entertaining
issue of intellectual sociology. In Schumpeter's case, nowhere better illus-
trated than in the core of *Capitalism, Socialism and Democracy* reprinted
here, the explanation that may suffice is simply that his was an act that was
extraordinarily difficult to follow. Although Schumpeter's intellectual hero
was Léon Walras, the great French inventor of general equilibrium theory,
his own canvas was far from a set of mathematical equations. Although
Schumpeter was a founder of the econometric society, he himself was an
indifferent mathematician. Those who appreciate literature can still enjoy
much of Schumpeter precisely because his subject was human history and
his analysis a blend of economic reasoning, historical analogy, aesthetic ap-
preciation, and perceptions as frequently political and sociological as nar-
rowly technical.

Schumpeter preferred to operate on the scale of the great works of the
eighteenth and nineteenth centuries—Adam Smith's *The Wealth of Nations*,
John Stuart Mill's *Principles of Political Economy*, and not least Karl
Marx's *Capital*. The authors of textbooks find it easy enough to simplify
and summarize the theory of competitive price. Following Paul Samuelson's
example, they have even succeeded in domesticating John Maynard Keynes,
by dint of discarding his historical speculations and converting what remained into a simple set of fiscal hydraulics.

Schumpeter resists bowdlerization. The vision is too subtle and the analysis too complex for primer translation. It is convenient here to consider the
argument of *Can Capitalism Survive?* Published in 1940, it appeared at a
time when Schumpeter's Harvard colleague Alvin Hansen, then a leading
American Keynesian, was popularizing a version of Keynes termed "secular
stagnation." In a famous 1938 address to the American Economic Association, Hansen maintained that capitalism was certain to suffer permanently
high unemployment, at least in the absence of government intervention,
because investment opportunity, the driving force of capitalist expansion,

had drastically diminished. In the American West the geographical frontier had closed. Population growth was slowing. And, for a number of reasons, new inventions and processes were likely to be less important in the future than they had been in the days of capitalist progress.

Schumpeter, a severe critic of Keynesian economics, dismissed this prognosis almost contemptuously. Those who comprehended business cycle history had no reason to be astounded by the economic calamities of the 1930s. According to Schumpeter, the Great Depression was neither more nor less than the trough of one of the majestic, fifty-year cycles in economic activity that marked the economic history of the West from the middle of the eighteenth century onward. Ample precedents existed even for the severity and duration of contemporary depression. If any novelty accompanied this latest episode it was simply the meddling of misguided politicians into natural processes of recovery and the consequent exacerbation and prolongation of the symptoms of economic pathology. For Keynesians, all of this sounded uncomfortably like Herbert Hoover. For the unemployed, it must have been scant consolation to be told that their condition was a part of the natural order.

But for his own reasons Schumpeter took a gloomier view of the future of capitalism than the secular stagnationists. The man was no comfort to the partisans of any received ideology. Capitalism was bound to fail precisely because of its own tremendous achievements. For Schumpeter, writing nearly a century later than Marx, capitalism was even more successful than Marx and Engels grudgingly conceded it to be in their 1848 *Communist Manifesto*. For the masses, standards of life had improved beyond the dreams of the eighteenth and nineteenth centuries. For nearly two hundred years, per capita output had risen steadily. Capitalism operates not primarily for the wealthy but by its nature mainly in the interests of the ordinary worker and his family. Capitalist productivity has shortened the workweek and conferred upon the masses the boon of leisure, which was formely the prerogative of rich and powerful elites. Cheap clothing, conveniently packaged food, and inexpensive home appliances are of no great consequence to the wealthy, who in every era can afford hordes of personal servants and the finest products of the most skilled craftsmen. In our own time (though happily not in Schumpeter's) television is an enormously cheap mass entertainment. By contrast, attendance at the opera cannot ever be cheap for no method known even to efficiency experts can improve the productivity of musicians and singers. Not even corporate contributors have found a way of doubling the speed at which the orchestra plays or halving the number of players.

For the common man, capitalism is the best of all systems. When it works well, it destroys old processes, technologies, and modes of organization. The new ones that capitalists substitute turn out larger and larger assortments of consumer goods and services for the largest possible number of customers. Of course, most businessmen, like most human beings, are timid creatures of limited imagination. The "gale of creative destruction," Schumpeter's term, is the work of a small minority—entrepreneurs of boldness and creativity who convert the inventions of scientists and engineers into items of pleasure for the customers and profit for the promoters. In sharp contrast to conventional professional wisdom Schumpeter had no fear that large corporations would stifle competition, retard innovation, or slow growth. Quite the contrary. It was the large corporation that subsidized research and development, not of course out of altruistic impulse but in the expectation of monopoly profits during the several years in which rivals sought frantically to catch up with new developments. Under capitalism, as Schumpeter diagnosed its behavior, progress is a matter of temporary monopoly and the brief spells of excess profits that such monopoly facilitates. But time and again new waves of innovation sweep over the flimsy barriers futilely erected by would-be monopolists. The lesson is not lost upon intelligent businessmen. Very alert and very successful giants in the corporate universe are completely aware that they can maintain their supremacy not by resting upon the laurels of present success but by running even faster in the direction of a still newer innovation, lest some rival get there first.

Schumpeter, who took a romantic view of capitalism, expected entrepreneurs to be aggressive "new" men, outsiders who scrambled for capital and opportunity. The typical entrepreneur was unlikely to be a second- or third-generation Morgan, Lodge, Cabot, or Rockefeller. It was far more likely that he would be an eccentric engineer like the first Henry Ford, a deaf tinkerer like Thomas Alva Edison, or an organizer of genius like John D. Rockefeller. These entrepreneurs were rarely if ever the scions of the best families, the graduates of Choate-Yale-Harvard Law School or their European equivalents. Entrepreneurs were drawn from the ranks of newcomers. The success of capitalism was inseparable from its capacity to enlist people of unusual talent and energy. The dynamism of capitalist performance was totally unconnected with the notions of delicate equilibrium in competitive markets over which legions of economists and their badgered students toiled. Capitalist progress was the consequence of the deliberate disruption, the departures from equilibrium that entrepreneurs repetitively introduced.

II

By any historical criterion capitalism was a great success. Yet when Schumpeter asked, "Can capitalism survive?" he promptly responded, "No. I do not think it can." Why not? Schumpeter greatly admired capitalism and sturdily detested socialism. What impelled him to predict defeat for the first and triumph for the second? Successful as capitalism has been, it is, in Schumpeter's judgment, a fragile form of organization dependent upon a protective environment and general popular support. In the very course of transforming the physical and social landscape and improving the common lot of its customers and employees, capitalism fatally damaged the sources of its stability and general acceptance. The very successes of capitalist organization diminished the role of the entrepreneur, the key figure in the drama of capitalist progress. Schumpeter mourned that invention had become a social process, a series of programmable products of group research controlled and financed by large corporations in great laboratories like those maintained by IBM, Bell Telephone, and their peers. Inventions are now made to order, marketed at the convenience of corporate executives, and guided by the mentality of cost accountants. The bold spirits whose élan shook up the world of conventional management in the heyday of capitalism are not wanted in the modern corporation. As the entrepreneurs of the past yield their places to salaried employees, the organization men of capitalism and the apparatchiks of socialism, the spirit of capitalism withers. Why should it matter to the average corporate executive whether his desk is owned by the Department of Defense or the Grumman Aircraft Corporation? The frequency of movement between government agencies and "private" corporations strongly implies that, just as Schumpeter asserted, the distinctions between public and private bureaucracies have become all but imperceptible.

Some of the sturdiest friends of capitalism are to be found not in large corporations but in smaller enterprises. The man or woman who runs a store or factory founded by his own sweat and thrift is bound to be warmly in favor of bourgeois capitalism. The large corporation persistently weakens the small bourgeoisie. In Schumpeter's words,

> . . . if capitalist evolution—"progress"—either ceases or becomes completely automatic, the economic basis of the industrial bourgeoisie will be reduced eventually to wages such as are paid for current administrative work. . . . Since capitalist enterprise, by its very achievements, tends to automatize progress, we conclude that it tends to make itself superfluous—to break to pieces under the pressure of its own success.

In the course of this self-destructive "progress,"

> the perfectly bureaucratized giant industrial unit not only ousts the small or medium-sized firm and "expropriates" its owners, but in the end it also ousts the entrepreneur and "expropriates" the bourgeoisie as a class which in the process stands to lose not only its income, but also what is infinitely more important, its function.

Marx rejoiced and Schumpeter wept at this prospect. The two, however, agreed that large units would triumph and small ones be destroyed. Marx

predicted a final crisis for capitalism because of the contradiction between
the tremendous productive capacity of large corporations and the limited
markets for their products that the inequities of capitalist distribution of
income and wealth allowed. According to Schumpeter, capitalism yields its
place on the historical stage essentially for sociological reasons. As a class,
capitalists will lose, perhaps already have lost, their *raison d'être*.

Schumpeter relished the irony of the circumstance that "the true pacemakers of socialism were not the intellectuals or agitators who preached it
but the Vanderbilts, Carnegies and Rockefellers." Of course, he added, "the
result may not in every respect be to the taste of Marxian socialists. . . . But
so far as prognosis goes, it does not differ from theirs."

Other historical trends also contribute to capitalism's demise. In their era
of glory, businessmen attended to their true vocation, the making of money,
and left politics and government to elites better qualified than themselves.
Royalty, clergy, and nobility protected traders in the dawn of capitalism, to
the substantial benefit of all parties. In England, a country Schumpeter
admired, "the aristocratic element continued to rule the roost *right to the
end of the period of intact and vital capitalism*" (italics in original). No great
admirer of political democracy, Schumpeter was convinced that the peaceful
governance of mankind required the skill and magic that businessmen,
clumsy and ineffective politicians one and all, notably lack. Businessmen can
add and subtract but "the stock exchange is a poor substitute for the Holy
Grail." The sad fact is that "economic leadership of this type does not readily
expand, like the medieval lord's leadership, into the leadership of nations."
Precisely because the bourgeois mentality is "rationalist" and "unheroic,"
businessmen who miscast themselves as statesmen defend their interests by
"rationalist and unheroic means" that must fail to "bend a nation." In sum,
"without protection by some non-bourgeois group, the bourgeoisie is politically helpless and unable not only to lead the nation but even to take care of
its own particular class interest." Paradoxical though it must sound, businessmen require a "master."

Unaware of their need, capitalists weaken and ultimately eliminate these
protecting social strata, "not only the king *Dei Gratia* but also the political
entrenchments that, had they proved tenable, would have been formed by
the village and the craft guild." Thus it is that the glories of capitalism, the
widening of markets to encompass the great globe itself and the substitution
of the calculus of profit maximization for traditional and traditionally un-
productive economic arrangements, are the occasion as well of the destruction of local squires, aristocrats, and monarchs whose natural charisma suited
them for the task of governance in the interests of capitalism.

In a curious way, Richard Nixon, who cannot justly be accused of reading
Schumpeter, perceived the necessity of mystery as an element of legitimacy.
Nixon's experiments with the details of presidential pomp and ceremony—

trumpeters in musical comedy uniforms, incessant performances of "Hail to the Chief," and ceremonial processions to Camp David, the "southern" White House, and the "western" White House—were invariably clumsy and frequently risible. Nevertheless, they were designed to supply some of the glamour notably absent in modern democracy and, if one believes Schumpeter, one of the sources of its malaise.

So far so bad, at least for a gloomy admirer of capitalism like Schumpeter. The entrepreneurial function is dying of inanition. Large corporations crowd out small capitalists. Having extinguished kings and aristocrats, businessmen turn awkwardly to the mysteries of public administration for which they lack talent. Schumpeter isolates still another way in which capitalism marches toward its own funeral. "The bourgeois fortress," now "politically defenseless," invites inevitable aggression.

Why should a set of economic arrangements beneficial to so many men and women incur their wrath? For one thing, the best arguments for capitalism focus on long-run achievement, the secular improvement in everyday life over which businessmen for two centuries at least have presided. Nobody lives to the age of two hundred. Ordinary human beings exist in the short run where such afflictions as job insecurity or actual unemployment diminish affection for capitalism. Life may be better for the clerk or factory operative than for his father, but he is tempted to contrast his modest income with the great fortunes accumulated by conspicuously successful businessmen. For most people the question is, what has capitalism done for me recently? Or, in Schumpeter's more dignified phrasing, "Secular improvement that is taken for granted and coupled with individual insecurity that is acutely resented is of course the best recipe for breeding social unrest."

The gnawing grievances and unfocused resentments of daily events require an energizing spark. This is the spark eagerly furnished by a group for which Schumpeter displays a highly controlled admiration—the intellectual community. As a social class, intellectuals are unique to capitalism, which "unlike any other type of society . . . inevitably and by virtue of the very logic of its civilization creates, educates and subsidizes a vested interest in social unrest." Although "a great part of their activities consists in fighting each other and in forming the spearheads of class interests not their own," intellectuals manage simultaneously to "develop group attitudes and group interests sufficiently strong to make large numbers of them behave in the way that is usually associated with the concept of social classes."

To put it mildly, intellectuals are a nuisance. Living by the written and spoken word, they lack the "first-hand knowledge" that only "actual experience" can generate. As envious onlookers, intellectuals are perpetually lured into uninformed criticism. Capitalism, which has fostered the printing press, universal literacy, and mass communication, has made the populace the patron of scribblers who once subsisted on the patronage of kings and courts

and behaved themselves accordingly. Higher education floods the land with
aspiring intellectuals and, despite the large market for vulgarized social
commentary and political analysis, the supply of aspiring purveyors of new
and borrowed intellectual nostrums is so copious that unemployment or
nonintellectual employment is the fate of many. There are simply too few
"intellectual" jobs, whether as writer, editor, or "communicator," to satisfy
the aspirations of intellectuals.

Mute poets and unpublished writers are predictably discontented. The
child of this emotion is resentment. Since it is bad form and inferior propaganda to generalize from individual disappointment, intellectual rage "often
rationalizes itself into that social criticism which . . . is in any case the intellectual spectator's typical attitude toward men, classes and institutions especially in a rationalist and utilitarian civilization." Intellectuals are a mis-
chievous class who corrupt the young, infiltrate trade unions, and jeer at the
simple patriotism of their fellow citizens.

How long can a social and economic system endure shorn of its political
protectors, fatally crippled by the erosion of the entrepreneurial function,
and buffeted by the assaults of ignorant but eloquent intellectuals? In his
more cheerful moods, Schumpeter gave capitalism a further run of one or
two generations, no more. Practically the last thing Schumpeter wrote, a
paper for the December 1949 meeting of the American Economic Association, focused on inflation as an accelerator of historical trends. If he were
alive now, he would presumably shorten his estimate of capitalist viability.

III

Despite the absence of a Schumpeterian school or even the sort of cult
that surrounds the memory of Thorstein Veblen, no great difficulty exists in
identifying the continuing influence of Schumpeter's central conception of
the nature and direction of capitalism. In the interests of brevity, I shall cite
three examples only. At a crucial point in his *The New Industrial State*,
John Kenneth Galbraith cites Schumpeter in the course of analyzing the
decline of entrepreneurship and the substitution of a "technostructure," a
word of Galbraith's coinage, of accountants, engineers, marketing analysts,
systems wizards, media manipulators, laboratory technicians, and assorted
allied experts who administer the large corporation after a fashion closely
resembling Schumpeter's sketch.

Daniel Bell in his recent *The Cultural Contradictions of Capitalism*
explicitly credits Schumpeter with a conception of the fiscal role of the state
that Bell converts into the idea of the public household. In Bell the central
clash between the economizing mode of thought that is the logic of capitalist production and the sociological style of mass consumption that empha-
sizes hedonism and instant impulse gratification appears to derive inspira-

tion from Schumpeter's evaluation of capitalism's self-destructive propensities.

Finally, the vein of pessimism that runs through Robert Heilbroner's *An Inquiry into the Human Condition* and his *The Decline of Business Civilization* echoes, though with significant variations, Schumpeter's dreary political projections. I do not state the case too strongly in asserting that those who indulge in general speculation about society are almost invariably driven to Marx and Schumpeter, however much they may differ from either or both of these powerful minds.

One guesses that the failure of mainstream economics to pay heed to his work would neither astound nor distress Schumpeter. By his lights, contemporary economics had been on the wrong track for some time. As economists specialized, they separated themselves from the analysis of society in which economics is only a bit player, seldom the star. As a subject, economics profited very little from overspecialization because the specialists concentrated less and less realistically on the nonexistent case of equilibrium under static conditions preferably of pure competition. But the defining characteristic of capitalism, according to Schumpeter, is disequilibrium. Accordingly, economic technicians are no more likely to comprehend social reality than hired administrators are capable of rescuing capitalism.

Unlike Marx, Schumpeter foresaw a peaceful march toward socialism. As a collector of taxes and dispenser of social bounty, the role of the state expands continually. As a vital enterprise, capitalism ineluctably declines into administrative routine. Is Jimmy Carter, a successful medium-sized capitalist, really going to preside over an American stroll into socialism? One shouldn't dismiss the possibility out of hand. In the light of traditional political categories, the United States is an extremely conservative society, devoted to free enterprise and unusually tolerant of its own millionaires. Michael Harrington's Democratic Socialist Organizing Committee numbers some 2,500 souls. The rival Social Democrats, U.S.A. is in a similar condition.

Such observations miss Schumpeter's point. The Carter energy program is an attempt to plan a vital sector of the economy to the tune of free enterprise incantation. Insofar as the White House succeeds, it will find itself guiding, planning, and influencing housing, public transportation, and the fifth of the economy associated with the production and servicing of automobiles. For all practical purposes the major defense contractors are public enterprises. Their condition became obvious when Congress voted public funds to keep Lockheed solvent. When capitalism was in flower, Lockheed would have been allowed to sink or swim without public attention.

Signs of the times are the acceptance of the notion of planning by respectable politicians and important business leaders. In 1976 Senators Javits and Humphrey introduced the National Economic Planning Act. The Humphrey-Hawkins Full Employment Bill is another stab at coordinated public planning. Neither bill has been enacted. What ought to intrigue and interest students of public affairs is the willingness of two orthodox liberals to boldly use the word "planning" and the endorsement of such a wild notion by tycoons like Treasury Secretary W. Michael Blumenthal, Henry Ford II, Felix Rohatyn, and Robert Roosa.

History, which often appears to be a string of jokes in dubious taste, may be about to perpetrate a new jape. Planning in the sense of an enlarged role for public activity is unlikely to fulfill the hopes and expectations of Marxists. Americans make poor revolutionaries and the phenomenon, as Marxists would say, of false class consciousness on the part of the proletariat is an open scandal. "Socialism," at least in its first guise, is certain to be little more than an easy transfer of business managers to Washington or, for that matter, a retitling of company presidents as government officials.

There are those who, not without reason, have suggested that mechanisms like the Emergency Financial Control Board and the Municipal Assistance Corporation, business-dominated agencies that for all practical purposes governed New York City during its spell of financial crisis, are essays in business socialism. The more alert members of the business and financial community already appear to have perceived that the best way to protect their interests is to socialize the risks of private enterprise while thoughtfully conserving the profits for their traditional recipients.

In all of this there is scant comfort either for radicals or celebrants of free markets. Only a Chicago-trained economist is likely to persist in the true competitive faith in a world of OPECs, aluminum cartels, state trading arrangements, third world demands for global redistribution, and export subsidy schemes of rich intricacy. The death of the free market is hardly tantamount to the expropriation of the wealthy or the hegemony of the working classes. In the perceptible future, Americans and Europeans are likely to continue to saunter into a version of business-controlled socialism, unlikely in the long run to be stable, but quite probably the shape of the next ten or twenty years.

Capitalism will be quietly transformed, so placidly that hardly a soul will notice. It is possible, theological arrangements permitting, that Schumpeter, wherever he is, will allow himself a quiet chuckle.

Robert Lekachman
Lehman College
City University of New York

Can Capitalism Survive?

PROLOGUE

CAN capitalism survive? No. I do not think it can. But this opinion of mine, like that of every other economist who has pronounced upon the subject, is in itself completely uninteresting. What counts in any attempt at social prognosis is not the Yes or No that sums up the facts and arguments which lead up to it but those facts and arguments themselves. They contain all that is scientific in the final result. Everything else is not science but prophecy. Analysis, whether economic or other, never yields more than a statement about the tendencies present in an observable pattern. And these never tell us what *will* happen to the pattern but only what *would* happen if they continued to act as they have been acting in the time interval covered by our observation and if no other factors intruded. "Inevitability" or "necessity" can never mean more than this.

What follows must be read with that proviso. But there are other limitations to our results and their reliability. The process of social life is a function of so many variables many of which are not amenable to anything like measurement that even mere diagnosis of a given state of things becomes a doubtful matter quite apart from the formidable sources of error that open up as soon as we attempt prognosis. These difficulties should not be exaggerated, however. We shall see that the dominant traits of the picture clearly support certain inferences which, whatever the qualifications that may have to be added, are too strong to be neglected on the ground that they cannot be proved in the sense in which a proposition of Euclid's can.

One more point before we start. The thesis I shall endeavor to establish is that the actual and prospective performance of the capitalist system is such as to negative the idea of its breaking down under the weight of economic failure, but that its very success undermines the social institutions which protect it, and "inevitably" creates conditions in which it will not be able to live and which strongly point to socialism as the heir apparent. My final conclusion therefore does not differ, however much my argument may, from that of most socialist writers and in particular from that of all Marxists. But in order to accept it one does not need to be a socialist. Prognosis does not imply anything about the desirability of the course of events that one predicts. If a doctor predicts that his patient will die presently, this does not mean that he desires it. One may hate socialism or at least look upon it with cool criticism, and yet foresee its advent. Many conservatives did and do.

Nor need one accept this conclusion in order to qualify as a social-ist. One may love socialism and ardently believe in its economic, cultural and ethical superiority but nevertheless believe at the same time that capitalist society does not harbor any tendency toward self-destruction. There are in fact socialists who believe that the capitalist order is gathering strength and is entrenching itself as time goes on, so that it is chimerical to hope for its breakdown.

I

THE RATE OF INCREASE OF TOTAL OUTPUT

THE atmosphere of hostility to capitalism which we shall have to explain presently makes it much more difficult than it otherwise would be to form a rational opinion about its economic and cultural performance. The public mind has by now so thoroughly grown out of humor with it as to make condemnation of capitalism and all its works a foregone conclusion—almost a requirement of the etiquette of discussion. Whatever his political preference, every writer or speaker hastens to conform to this code and to emphasize his critical attitude, his freedom from "complacency," his belief in the inadequacies of capitalist achievement, his aversion to capitalist and his sympathy with anti-capitalist interests. Any other attitude is voted not only foolish but anti-social and is looked upon as an indication of immoral servitude. This is of course perfectly natural. New social religions will always have that effect. Only it does not make it easier to fulfill the analyst's task: in 300 A.D. it would not have been easy to expound the achievements of ancient civilization to a fervent believer in Christianity. On the one hand, the most obvious truths are simply put out of court *a limine*;[1] on the other hand, the most obvious misstatements are borne with or applauded.

A first test of economic performance is total output, the total of all the commodities and services produced in a unit of time—a year or a quarter of a year or a month. Economists try to measure variations in this quantity by means of indices derived from a number of series representing the output of individual commodities. "Strict logic is a stern master, and if one respected it, one would never construct or use any production index,"[2] for not only the material and the technique of constructing such an index, but the very concept of a total output of different commodities produced in ever-changing proportions, is a highly doubtful matter.[3] Nevertheless, I believe that this device is sufficiently reliable to give us a general idea.

[1] There is however another method of dealing with obvious though uncomfortable truth, viz., the method of sneering at its triviality. Such a sneer will serve as well as a refutation would, for the average audience is as a rule perfectly unaware of the fact that it often covers the impossibility of denial—a pretty specimen of social psychology.

[2] A. F. Burns, *Production Trends in the United States Since 1870*, p. 262.

[3] We cannot enter into this problem here. A little will, however, be said about it when we meet it again in the next chapter. For a fuller treatment see my book on *Business Cycles*, ch. ix.

For the United States, individual series good and numerous enough
to warrant construction of such an index of output are available since
the Civil War. Choosing what is known as the Day-Persons index of
total production[4] we find that, from 1870 to 1930, the average annual
rate of growth was 3.7 per cent and, in the division of manufactures
alone, 4.3 per cent. Let us concentrate on the former figure and try
to visualize what it means. In order to do this we must first apply a
correction: since the durable equipment of industry was always increasing in relative importance, output available for consumption
cannot have increased at the same rate as total production. We must
allow for that. But I believe that an allowance of 1.7 per cent is
ample;[5] thus we arrive at a rate of increase in "available output" of 2
per cent (compound interest) per year.

Now suppose that the capitalist engine keeps on producing at that
rate of increase for another half century starting from 1928. To this assumption there are various objections which will have to be noticed
later on, but it cannot be objected to on the ground that in the decade
from 1929 to 1939 capitalism had already failed to live up to that standard. For the depression that ran its course from the last quarter of 1929
to the third quarter of 1932 does not prove that a secular break has
occurred in the propelling mechanism of capitalist production because depressions of such severity have repeatedly occurred—roughly
once in fifty-five years—and because the effects of one of them—the
one from 1873 to 1877—are taken account of in the annual average
of 2 per cent. The subnormal recovery to 1935, the subnormal prosperity to 1937 and the slump after that are easily accounted for by
the difficulties incident to the adaptation to a new fiscal policy, new
labor legislation and a general change in the attitude of government
to private enterprise all of which can, in a sense to be defined later, be
distinguished from the working of the productive apparatus as such.

Since misunderstandings at this point would be especially undesir-
able, I wish to emphasize that the last sentence does not in itself
imply either an adverse criticism of the New Deal policies or the proposition—which I do believe to be true but which I do not need just
now—that policies of that type are in the long run incompatible with
the effective working of the system of private enterprise. All I now
mean to imply is that so extensive and rapid a change of the social
scene naturally affects productive performance for a time, and so
much the most ardent New Dealer must *and also can* admit. I for one
do not see how it would otherwise be possible to account for the

[4] See W. M. Persons, *Forecasting Business Cycles,* ch. xi.

[5] That allowance is in fact absurdly large. See also Professor F. C. Mill's estimate
of 3.1 per cent for the period 1901-1913, and of 3.8 per cent for the period 1922-
1929 (construction excluded; *Economic Tendencies in the United States,* 1932).

fact that this country which had the best chance of recovering quickly was precisely the one to experience the most unsatisfactory recovery. The only somewhat similar case, that of France, supports the same inference. It follows that the course of events during the decade from 1929 to 1939 does not *per se* constitute a valid reason for refusing to listen to the argument in hand which, moreover, may in any case serve to illustrate the meaning of past performance.

Well, if from 1928 on available production under the conditions of the capitalist order continued to develop as it did before, i.e., at a long-run average rate of increase of 2 per cent per year, it would after fifty years, in 1978, reach an amount of roughly 2.7 (2.6916) times the 1928 figure. In order to translate this into terms of average real income *per head of population*, we first observe that our rate of increase in total output may be roughly equated to the rate of increase in the sum total of private money incomes available for consumption,[6] corrected for changes in the purchasing power of the consumers' dollars. Second, we must form an idea about the increase in population we are to expect; we will choose Mr. Sloane's estimate, which gives 160 millions for 1978. Average income per head during those fifty years would therefore increase to a little more than double its 1928 amount, which was about $650, or to about $1300 *of 1928 purchasing power*.[7]

Perhaps some readers feel that a proviso should be added about the distribution of the total monetary income. Until about forty years ago, many economists besides Marx believed that the capitalist process tended to change relative shares in the national total so that the obvious inference from our average might be invalidated by the rich growing richer and the poor growing poorer, at least relatively. But there is no such tendency. Whatever may be thought of the statistical measures devised for the purpose, this much is certain: that the structure of the pyramid of incomes, expressed in terms of money, has not greatly changed during the period covered by our material

[6] "Consumption" includes the acquisition of durable consumers' goods such as motor cars, refrigerators and homes. We do not distinguish between transient consumers' goods and what is sometimes referred to as "consumers' capital."

[7] That is to say, average real income per head would increase at a compound interest rate of 1⅜ per cent. It so happens that in England, during the century preceding the First World War, real income per head of population increased at almost exactly that rate (see Lord Stamp in *Wealth and Taxable Capacity*). No great confidence can be placed in this coincidence. But I think it serves to show that our little calculation is not wildly absurd. In Number 241 of the *National Industrial Conference Board Studies*, Table I, pp. 6 and 7, we find that "per capita realized national income" adjusted by the Federal Reserve Bank of New York and the National Industrial Conference Board cost of living index, was in 1929 a little over four times the 1829 figure—a similar result, though open to still more serious doubts as to reliability.

—which for England includes the whole of the nineteenth century[8] —and that the relative share of wages plus salaries has also been substantially constant over time. There is, so long as we are discussing what the capitalist engine might do if left to itself, no reason to believe that the distribution of incomes or the dispersion about our average would in 1978 be significantly different from what it was in 1928.

One way of expressing our result is that, if capitalism repeated its past performance for another half century starting with 1928, this would do away with anything that according to present standards could be called poverty, even in the lowest strata of the population, pathological cases alone excepted.

Nor is this all. Whatever else our index may do or may not do, it certainly does not overstate the actual rate of increase. It does not take account of the commodity, Voluntary Leisure. New commodities escape or are inadequately represented by an index which must rest largely on basic commodities and intermediate products. For the same reason improvements in quality almost completely fail to assert themselves although they constitute, in many lines, the core of the progress achieved—there is no way of expressing adequately the difference between a motorcar of 1940 and a motorcar of 1900 or the extent to which the price of motorcars per unit of utility has fallen. It would be more nearly possible to estimate the rate at which given quantities of raw materials or semi-finished products are made to go further than they used to—a steel ingot or a ton of coal, though they may be unchanged in physical quality, represent a multiple of their economic efficiency sixty years ago. But little has been done along this line. I have no idea about what would happen to our index if there were a method for correcting it for these and similar factors. It is certain, however, that its percentage rate of change would be increased and that we have here a reserve that should make the estimate adopted proof against the effects of any conceivable downward revision. Moreover, even if we had the means of measuring the change in the technological efficiency of industrial products, this measure would still fail to convey an adequate idea of what it means for the dignity or intensity or pleasantness of human life—for all that the economists of an earlier generation subsumed under the heading of Satisfaction of Wants. And this, after all, is for us the relevant consideration, the true "output" of capitalist production, the reason

---

[8] See Stamp, *op. cit.* The same phenomenon can be observed in all countries for which there is sufficient statistical information, if we clear the latter of the disturbing effect of the cycles of various span that are covered by the available material. The measure of income distribution (or of inequality of incomes) devised by Vilfredo Pareto is open to objection. But the fact itself is independent of its shortcomings.

why we are interested in the index of production and the pounds and gallons that enter into it and would hardly be worth while in themselves.

But let us keep to our 2 per cent. There is one more point that is important for a correct appraisal of that figure. I have stated above that, broadly speaking, relative shares in national income have remained substantially constant over the last hundred years. This, however, is true only if we measure them in money. Measured in real terms, relative shares have substantially changed in favor of the lower income groups. This follows from the fact that the capitalist engine is first and last an engine of mass production which unavoidably means also production for the masses, whereas, climbing upward in the scale of individual incomes, we find that an increasing proportion is being spent on personal services and on handmade commodities, the prices of which are largely a function of wage rates.

Verification is easy. There are no doubt some things available to the modern workman that Louis XIV himself would have been delighted to have yet was unable to have—modern dentistry for instance. On the whole, however, a budget on that level had little that really mattered to gain from capitalist achievement. Even speed of traveling may be assumed to have been a minor consideration for so very dignified a gentleman. Electric lighting is no great boon to anyone who has money enough to buy a sufficient number of candles and to pay servants to attend to them. It is the cheap cloth, the cheap cotton and rayon fabric, boots, motorcars and so on that are the typical achievements of capitalist production, and not as a rule improvements that would mean much to the rich man. Queen Elizabeth owned silk stockings. The capitalist achievement does not typically consist in providing more silk stockings for queens but in bringing them within the reach of factory girls in return for steadily decreasing amounts of effort.

The same fact stands out still better if we glance at those long waves in economic activity, analysis of which reveals the nature and mechanism of the capitalist process better than anything else. Each of them consists of an "industrial revolution" and the absorption of its effects. For instance, we are able to observe statistically and historically—the phenomenon is so clear that even our scanty information suffices to establish it—the rise of such a long wave toward the end of the 1780's, its culmination around 1800, its downward sweep and then a sort of recovery ending at the beginning of the 1840's. This was the Industrial Revolution dear to the heart of textbook writers. Upon its heels, however, came another such revolution producing another long wave that rose in the forties, culminated just before 1857 and ebbed away to 1897, to be followed in turn by the one that reached its peak about 1911 and is now in the act of ebbing away.[9]

These revolutions periodically reshape the existing structure of industry by introducing new methods of production—the mechanized factory, the electrified factory, chemical synthesis and the like; new commodities, such as railroad service, motorcars, electrical appliances; new forms of organization—the merger movement; new sources of supply—La Plata wool, American cotton, Katanga copper; new trade routes and markets to sell in and so on. This process of industrial change provides the ground swell that gives the general tone to business: while these things are being initiated we have brisk expenditure and predominating "prosperity"—interrupted, no doubt, by the negative phases of the shorter cycles that are superimposed on that ground swell—and while those things are being completed and their results pour forth we have elimination of antiquated elements of the industrial structure and predominating "depression." Thus there are prolonged periods of rising and of falling prices, interest rates, employment and so on, which phenomena constitute parts of the mechanism of this process of recurrent rejuvenation of the productive apparatus.

Now these results each time consist in an avalanche of consumers' goods that permanently deepens and widens the stream of real income although in the first instance they spell disturbance, losses and unemployment. And if we look at those avalanches of consumers' goods we again find that each of them consists in articles of mass consumption and increases the purchasing power of the wage dollar more than that of any other dollar—in other words, that the capitalist process, not by coincidence but by virtue of its mechanism, progressively raises the standard of life of the masses. It does so through a sequence of vicissitudes, the severity of which is proportional to the speed of the advance. But it does so effectively. One problem after another of the supply of commodities to the masses has been successfully solved[10] by being brought within the reach of the methods of capitalist production. The most important one of those that remain, housing, is approaching solution by means of the pre-fabricated house.

And still this is not all. Appraisal of an economic order would be incomplete—and incidentally un-Marxian—if it stopped at the output which the corresponding economic conveyor hands to the various groups of society and left out of account all those things that the conveyor does not serve directly but for which it provides the means

[9] These are the "long waves" which, in business cycle literature, are primarily associated with the name of N. D. Kondratieff.

[10] This of course also applies to agricultural commodities, the cheap mass production of which was entirely the work of large-scale capitalist enterprise (railroads, shipping, agricultural machinery, fertilizers).

as well as the political volition, and all those cultural achievements
that are induced by the mentality it generates. Deferring consideration of the latter (Chapter VII), we shall now turn to some aspects
of the former.

The technique and atmosphere of the struggle for social legislation
obscures the otherwise obvious facts that, on the one hand, part of
this legislation presupposes previous capitalist success (in other words,
wealth which had previously to be created by capitalist enterprise)
and that, on the other hand, much of what social legislation develops
and generalizes had been previously initiated by the action of the capitalist stratum itself. Both facts must of course be added to the sum
total of capitalist performance. Now if the system had another run
such as it had in the sixty years preceding 1928 and really reached
the $1300 *per head of population,* it is easy to see that all the de-
siderata that have so far been espoused by any social reformers—
practically without exception, including even the greater part of the
cranks—either would be fulfilled automatically or could be fulfilled
without significant interference with the capitalist process. Ample
provision for the unemployed in particular would then be not
only a tolerable but a light burden. Irresponsibility in creating unemployment and in financing the support of the unemployed might
of course at any time create insoluble problems. But managed with
ordinary prudence, an *average* annual expenditure of 16 billions
on an *average* number of 16 million unemployed including dependents (10 per cent of the population) would not in itself be a serious
matter with an available national income of the order of magnitude
of 200 billion dollars (purchasing power of 1928).

May I call the reader's attention to the reason why unemployment
which everyone agrees must be one of the most important issues in
any discussion of capitalism—with some critics so much so that they
base their indictment exclusively on this element of the case—will play
a comparatively small role in my argument? I do not think that unemployment is among those evils which, like poverty, capitalist evolution could ever eliminate of itself. I also do not think that there
is any tendency for the unemployment percentage to increase in the
long run. The only series covering a respectable time interval—
roughly the sixty years preceding the First World War—gives the English trade-union percentage of unemployed members. It is a typically
cyclical series and displays no trend (or a horizontal one).[11] Since this
is theoretically understandable—there is no theoretical reason to call
the evidence in question—those two propositions seem established for

---

[11] That series has often been charted and analyzed. See for instance, A. C. Pigou,
Industrial Fluctuations or my *Business Cycles.* For every country there seems to
be an irreducible minimum and, superimposed on that, a cyclical movement, the
strongest component of which has a period of about nine to ten years.

the prewar time to 1913 inclusive. In the postwar time and in most countries unemployment was mostly at an abnormally high level even before 1930. But this and still more the unemployment during the thirties can be accounted for on grounds that have nothing to do with a long-run tendency of unemployment percentages to increase *from causes inherent in the capitalist mechanism itself*. I have mentioned above those industrial revolutions which are so characteristic of the capitalist process. Supernormal unemployment is one of the features of the periods of adaptation that follow upon the "prosperity phase" of each of them. We observe it in the 1820's and 1870's, and the period after 1920 is simply another of those periods. So far the phenomenon is essentially temporary in the sense that nothing can be inferred about it for the future. But there were a number of other factors which tended to intensify it—war effects, dislocations of foreign trade, wage policies, certain institutional changes that swelled the statistical figure, in England and Germany fiscal policies (also important in the United States since 1935) and so on. Some of these are no doubt symptoms of an "atmosphere" in which capitalism will work with decreasing efficiency. That however is another matter which will engage our attention later on.

But whether lasting or temporary, getting worse or not, unemployment undoubtedly is and always has been a scourge. In the next part of this book we shall have to list its possible elimination among the claims of the socialist order to superiority. Nevertheless, I hold that the real tragedy is not unemployment *per se*, but unemployment plus the impossibility of providing adequately for the unemployed *without impairing the conditions of further economic development*: for obviously the suffering and degradation—the destruction of human values—which we associate with unemployment, though not the waste of productive resources, would be largely eliminated and unemployment would lose practically all its terror if the private life of the unemployed were not seriously affected by their unemployment. The indictment stands that in the past—say, roughly, to the end of the nineteenth century—the capitalist order was not only unwilling but also quite incapable of guaranteeing this. But since it will be able to do so if it keeps up its past performance for another half century this indictment would in that case enter the limbo filled by the sorry specters of child labor and sixteen-hour working days and five persons living in one room which it is quite proper to emphasize when we are talking about the past social costs of capitalist achievement but which are not necessarily relevant to the balance of alternatives for the future. Our own time is somewhere between the disabilities of earlier stages in capitalist evolution and the abilities of the system in full maturity. In this country at least, the better part of the task could even now be accomplished without undue strain on the system. The difficulties do not seem to consist so much in the lack of a surplus sufficient to blot out the darkest hues in the picture: they consist, on the one hand, in the fact that the unemployment figure has been increased by anti-capitalist policies beyond what it need have been in the thirties and, on the other hand, in the fact that public opinion as soon as it becomes at all alive to the duty in question, immediately insists on economically irrational methods of financing relief and on lax and wasteful methods of administering it.

Much the same argument applies to the future—and to a great extent the present—possibilities held out by capitalist evolution for the care of the aged and sick, for education and hygiene and so on. Also, an increasing number of commodities might reasonably be expected, from the standpoint of the individual household, to pass out of the class of economic goods and to be available practically up to the satiety point. This could be brought about either by arrangements between public agencies and producing concerns or by nationalization or municipalization, gradual progress with which would of course be a feature of the future development even of an otherwise unfettered capitalism.

II

PLAUSIBLE CAPITALISM

THE argument of the preceding chapter seems to be exposed to a reply that is as damaging as it is obvious. The average rate of increase in total available production that obtained during the sixty years preceding 1928 has been projected into the future. So far as this was merely a device in order to illustrate the significance of past development, there was nothing in this procedure that could have shocked the statistical conscience. But as soon as I implied that the following fifty years might actually display a similar average rate of increase, I apparently did commit a statistical crime; it is, of course, clear that a historical record of production over any given period does not in itself justify any extrapolation at all,[1] let alone an extrapolation over half a century. It is therefore necessary to emphasize again that my extrapolation is not intended to forecast the actual behavior of output in the future. Beyond illustrating the meaning of past performance, it is merely intended to give us a quantitative idea of what the capitalist engine might conceivably accomplish if, for another half century, it repeated its past performance—which is a very different matter. The question whether it can be expected to do so will be answered quite independently of the extrapolation itself. For this purpose we have now to embark upon a long and difficult investigation.

Before we can discuss the chance of capitalism repeating its past performance we must evidently try to find out in what sense the observed rate of increase in output really measures that past performance. No doubt, the period that furnished our data was one of comparatively unfettered capitalism. But this fact does not in itself provide a sufficient link between the performance and the capitalist engine. In order to believe that this was more than coincidence we must satisfy ourselves first, that there is an understandable relation between the capitalist order and the observed rate of increase in output; second, that, given such a relation, the rate of increase was actually due to it and not to

---

[1] This proposition holds, on general principles, for any *historical* time series, since the very concept of historical sequence implies the occurrence of irreversible changes in the economic structure which must be expected to affect the law of any given economic quantity. Theoretical justification and, as a rule, statistical treatment are therefore necessary for even the most modest extrapolations. It may however be urged that our case is somewhat favored by the fact that within the comprehensive compound represented by the output series, idiosyncrasies of individual items will to some extent cancel each other.

particularly favorable conditions which had nothing to do with capitalism.

These two problems must be solved before the problem of a "repetition of performance" can arise at all. The third point then reduces to the question whether there is any reason why the capitalist engine should, during the next forty years, fail to go on working as it did in the past.

We shall deal with these three points in turn.

Our first problem may be reformulated as follows. On the one hand, we have a considerable body of statistical data descriptive of a rate of "progress" that has been admired even by very critical minds. On the other hand, we have a body of facts about the structure of the economic system of that period and about the way it functioned; from these facts, analysis has distilled what is technically called a "model" of capitalist reality, i.e., a generalized picture of its essential features. We wish to know whether that type of economy was favorable, irrelevant, or unfavorable to the performance we observe and, if favorable, whether those features may be reasonably held to yield adequate explanation of this performance. Waiving technicalities as much as possible, we shall approach the question in a common-sense spirit.

1. Unlike the class of feudal lords, the commercial and industrial bourgeoisie rose by business success. Bourgeois society has been cast in a purely economic mold: its foundations, beams and beacons are all made of economic material. The building faces toward the economic side of life. Prizes and penalties are measured in pecuniary terms. Going up and going down means making and losing money. This, of course, nobody can deny. But I wish to add that, within its own frame, that social arrangement is, or at all events was, singularly effective. In part it appeals to, and in part it creates, a schema of motives that is unsurpassed in simplicity and force. The promises of wealth and the threats of destitution that it holds out, it redeems with ruthless promptitude. Wherever the bourgeois way of life asserts itself sufficiently to dim the beacons of other social worlds, these promises are strong enough to attract the large majority of supernormal brains and to identify success with business success. They are not proffered at random; yet there is a sufficiently enticing admixture of chance: the game is not like roulette, it is more like poker. They are addressed to ability, energy and supernormal capacity for work; but if there were a way of measuring either that ability in general or the personal achievement that goes into any particular success, the premiums actually paid out would probably not be found proportional to either. Spectacular prizes much greater than would have been necessary to call forth the particular effort are thrown to a small minority of winners, thus propelling much more efficaciously than a

more equal and more "just" distribution would, the activity of that large majority of businessmen who receive in return very modest compensation or nothing or less than nothing, and yet do their utmost because they have the big prizes before their eyes and overrate their chances of doing equally well. Similarly, the threats are addressed to incompetence. But though the incompetent men and the obsolete methods are in fact eliminated, sometimes very promptly, sometimes with a lag, failure also threatens or actually overtakes many an able man, thus whipping up *everyone*, again much more efficaciously than a more equal and more "just" system of penalties would. Finally, both business success and business failure are ideally precise. Neither can be talked away.

One aspect of this should be particularly noticed, for future reference as well as because of its importance for the argument in hand. In the way indicated and also in other ways which will be discussed later on, the capitalist arrangement, as embodied in the institution of private enterprise, effectively chains the bourgeois stratum to its tasks. But it does more than that. The same apparatus which conditions for performance the individuals and families that at any given time form the bourgeois class, *ipso facto* also selects the individuals and families that are to rise into that class or to drop out of it. This combination of the conditioning and the selective function is not a matter of course. On the contrary, most methods of social selection, unlike the "methods" of biological selection, do not guarantee performance of the selected individual; and their failure to do so constitutes one of the crucial problems of socialist organization that will come up for discussion at another stage of our inquiry. For the time being, it should merely be observed how well the capitalist system solves that problem: in most cases the man who rises first *into* the business class and then *within* it is also an able businessman and he is likely to rise exactly as far as his ability goes—simply because in that schema rising to a position and doing well in it generally is or was one and the same thing. This fact, so often obscured by the auto-therapeutic effort of the unsuccessful to deny it, is much more important for an appraisal of capitalist society and its civilization than anything that can be gleaned from the pure theory of the capitalist machine.

2. But is not all that we might be tempted to infer from "maximum performance of an optimally selected group" invalidated by the further fact that that performance is not geared to social service—production, so we might say, for consumption—but to money-making, that it aims at maximizing profits instead of welfare? Outside of the bourgeois stratum, this has of course always been the popular opinion. Economists have sometimes fought and sometimes espoused it. In doing so they have contributed something that was much more valuable than were the final judgments themselves at which they arrived

individually and which in most cases reflect little more than their social location, interests and sympathies or antipathies. They slowly increased our factual knowledge and analytic powers so that the answers to many questions we are able to give today are no doubt much more correct although less simple and sweeping than were those of our predecessors.

To go no further back, the so-called classical economists[2] were practically of one mind. Most of them disliked many things about the social institutions of their epoch and about the way those institutions worked. They fought the landed interest and approved of social reforms—factory legislation in particular—that were not all on the lines of *laissez faire*. But they were quite convinced that within the institutional framework of capitalism, the manufacturer's and the trader's self-interest made for maximum performance in the interest of all. Confronted with the problem we are discussing, they would have had little hesitation in attributing the observed rate of increase in total output to relatively unfettered enterprise and the profit motive —perhaps they would have mentioned "beneficial legislation" as a condition but by this they would have meant the removal of fetters, especially the removal or reduction of protective duties during the nineteenth century.

It is exceedingly difficult, at this hour of the day, to do justice to these views. They were of course the typical views of the English bourgeois class, and bourgeois blinkers are in evidence on almost every page the classical authors wrote. No less in evidence are blinkers of another kind: the classics reasoned in terms of a particular historical situation which they uncritically idealized and from which they un-critically generalized. Most of them, moreover, seem to have argued exclusively in terms of the English interests and problems of their time. This is the reason why, in other lands and at other times, people disliked their economics, frequently to the point of not even caring to understand it. But it will not do to dismiss their teaching on these grounds. A prejudiced man may yet be speaking the truth. Propositions developed from special cases may yet be generally valid. And the enemies and successors of the classics had and have only different but not fewer blinkers and preconceptions; they envisaged and envisage different but not less special cases.

From the standpoint of the economic analyst, the chief merit of the classics consists in their dispelling, along with many other gross errors, the naïve idea that economic activity in capitalist society, because it

[2] The term Classical Economists will in this book be used to designate the leading English economists whose works appeared between 1776 and 1848. Adam Smith, Ricardo, Malthus, Senior and John Stuart Mill are the outstanding names. It is important to keep this in mind because a much broader use of the term has come into fashion of late.

turns on the profit motive, must by virtue of that fact alone necessarily run counter to the interests of consumers; or, to put it differently, that moneymaking necessarily deflects producing from its social goal; or, finally, that private profits, both in themselves and through the distortion of the economic process they induce, are always a net loss to all excepting those who receive them and would therefore constitute a net gain to be reaped by socialization. If we look at the logic of these and similar propositions which no trained economist ever thought of defending, the classical refutation may well seem trivial. But as soon as we look at all the theories and slogans which, consciously or subconsciously, imply them and which are once more served up today, we shall feel more respect for that achievement. Let me add at once that the classical writers also clearly perceived, though they may have exaggerated, the role of saving and accumulation and that they linked saving to the rate of "progress" they observed in a manner that was fundamentally, if only approximately, correct. Above all, there was practical wisdom about their doctrine, a responsible long-run view and a manly tone that contrast favorably with modern hysterics.

But between realizing that hunting for a maximum of profit and striving for maximum productive performance are not necessarily incompatible, to proving that the former will necessarily—or in the immense majority of cases—imply the latter, there is a gulf much wider than the classics thought. And they never succeeded in bridging it. The modern student of their doctrines never ceases to wonder how it was possible for them to be satisfied with their arguments or to mistake these arguments for proofs; in the light of later analysis their *theory* was seen to be a house of cards whatever measure of truth there may have been in their *vision*.[3]

3. This later analysis we will take in two strides—as much of it, that is, as we need in order to clarify our problem. Historically, the first will carry us into the first decade of this century, the second will cover some of the postwar developments of scientific economics. Frankly I do not know how much good this will do the non-professional reader; like every other branch of our knowledge, economics, as its analytic engine improves, moves fatally away from that happy stage in which all problems, methods and results could be made accessible to every educated person without special training. I will, however, do my best.

The first stride may be associated with two great names revered to

[3] The reader will recall my emphasis on the distinction between one's theory and one's vision in the case of Marx. It is however always important to remember that the ability to see things in their correct perspective may be, and often is, divorced from the ability to reason correctly and vice versa. That is why a man may be a very good theorist and yet talk absolute nonsense whenever confronted with the task of diagnosing a concrete historical pattern as a whole.

this day by numberless disciples—so far at least as the latter do not think it bad form to express reverence for anything or anybody, which many of them obviously do—Alfred Marshall and Knut Wicksell.[4] Their theoretical structure has little in common with that of the classics—though Marshall did his best to hide the fact—but it conserves the classic proposition that in the case of perfect competition the profit interest of the producer tends to maximize production. It even supplied almost satisfactory proof. Only, in the process of being more correctly stated and proved, the proposition lost much of its content—it does emerge from the operation, to be sure, but it emerges emaciated, barely alive.[5] Still it can be shown, within the general assumptions of the Marshall-Wicksell analysis, that firms which cannot by their own individual action exert any influence upon the price of their products or of the factors of production they employ—so that there would be no point in their weeping over the fact that any increase in production tends to decrease the former and to increase the latter—will expand their output until they reach the point at which the additional cost that must be incurred in order to produce another small increment of product (marginal cost) just equals the price they

---

[4] Marshall's *Principles* (first edition 1890) and Wicksell's *Lectures* (first Swedish edition 1901, English translation 1934) are entitled to the prominence I am here giving to them, because of the influence they exerted on many minds in their formative stages and because they dealt with theory in a thoroughly practical spirit. On purely scientific grounds, precedence should be given to the work of Léon Walras. In America, the names to mention are J. B. Clark, Irving Fisher and F. W. Taussig.

[5] Anticipating later argument (see below, ch. iv, § 6) I shall in this note briefly clarify the above passage. Analysis of the mechanism of the profit economy led not only to the discovery of exceptions to the principle that competitive industry tends to maximize output, but also to the discovery that proof of the principle itself requires assumptions which reduce it to little more than a truism. Its practical value is however particularly impaired by the two following considerations:

1. The principle, as far as it can be proved at all, applies to a state of static equilibrium. Capitalist reality is first and last a process of change. In appraising the performance of competitive enterprise, the question whether it would or would not tend to maximize production in a perfectly equilibrated stationary condition of the economic process is hence almost, though not quite, irrelevant.

2. The principle, as stated by Wicksell, is what was left of a more ambitious proposition that, though in a rarefied form, can still be found in Marshall—the theorem that competitive industry tends to produce a state of maximum satisfaction of wants. But this theorem, even if we waive the serious objections to speaking of non-observable psychic magnitudes, is readily seen to boil down to the triviality that, whatever the data and in particular the institutional arrangements of a society may be, human action, as far as it is rational, will always try to make the best of any given situation. In fact it boils down to a definition of rational action and can hence be paralleled by analogous theorems for, say, a socialist society. But so can the principle of maximum production. Neither formulates any specific virtue of private competitive enterprise. This does not mean that such virtues do not exist. It does mean however that they are not simply inherent in the *logic* of competition.

can get for that increment, i.e., that they will produce as much as they can without running into loss. And this can be shown to be as much as it is in general "socially desirable" to produce. In more technical language, in that case prices are, from the standpoint of the individual firm, not variables but parameters; and where this is so, there exists a state of equilibrium in which all outputs are at their maximum and all factors fully employed. This case is usually referred to as perfect competition. Remembering what has been said about the selective process which operates on all firms and their managers, we might in fact conceive a very optimistic idea of the results to be expected from a highly selected group of people forced, within that pattern, by their profit motive to strain every nerve in order to maximize output and to minimize costs. In particular, it might seem at first sight that a system conforming to this pattern would display remarkable absence of some of the major sources of social waste. As a little reflection should show, this is really but another way of stating the content of the preceding sentence.

4. Let us take the second stride. The Marshall-Wicksell analysis of course did not overlook the many cases that fail to conform to that model. Nor, for that matter, had the classics overlooked them. They recognized cases of "monopoly," and Adam Smith himself carefully noticed the prevalence of devices to restrict competition[6] and all the differences in flexibility of prices resulting therefrom. But they looked upon those cases as exceptions and, moreover, as exceptions that could and would be done away with in time. Something of that sort is true also of Marshall. Although he developed the Cournot theory of monopoly[7] and although he anticipated later analysis by calling attention to the fact that most firms have special markets of their own in which they set prices instead of merely accepting them,[8] he as well as Wicksell framed his general conclusions on the pattern of perfect competition so as to suggest, much as the classics did, that perfect competition was the rule. Neither Marshall and Wicksell nor the classics saw that perfect competition is the exception and that even if it were the rule there would be much less reason for congratulation than one might think.

If we look more closely at the conditions—not all of them explicitly stated or even clearly seen by Marshall and Wicksell—that must be fulfilled in order to produce perfect competition, we realize imme-

---

[6] In a manner strikingly suggestive of present-day attitudes he even emphasized the discrepancy between the interests of every trade and those of the public and talked about conspiracies against the latter which, so he thought, might originate at any businessmen's dinner party.

[7] Augustin Cournot, 1938.

[8] This is why the later theory of imperfect competition may fairly be traced to him. Though he did not elaborate it, he saw the phenomenon more correctly than most of those who did. In particular he did not exaggerate its importance.

diately that outside of agricultural mass production there cannot be many instances of it. A farmer supplies his cotton or wheat in fact under those conditions: from his standpoint the ruling prices of cotton or wheat are data, though very variable ones, and not being able to influence them by his individual action he simply adapts his output; since all farmers do the same, prices and quantities will in the end be adjusted as the theory of perfect competition requires. But this is not so even with many agricultural products—with ducks, sausages, vegetables and many dairy products for instance. And as regards practically all the finished products and services of industry and trade, it is clear that every grocer, every filling station, every manufacturer of gloves or shaving cream or handsaws has a small and precarious market of his own which he tries—must try—to build up and to keep by price strategy, quality strategy—"product differentiation"—and advertising. Thus we get a completely different pattern which there seems to be no reason to expect to yield the results of perfect competition and which fits much better into the monopolistic schema. In these cases we speak of Monopolistic Competition. Their theory has been one of the major contributions to postwar economics.[9]

There remains a wide field of substantially homogeneous products —mainly industrial raw materials and semi-finished products such as steel ingots, cement, cotton gray goods and the like—in which the conditions for the emergence of monopolistic competition do not seem to prevail. This is so. But in general, similar results follow for that field inasmuch as the greater part of it is covered by largest-scale firms which, either individually or in concert, are able to manipulate prices even without differentiating products—the case of Oligopoly. Again the monopoly schema, suitably adapted, seems to fit this type of behavior much better than does the schema of perfect competition.

As soon as the prevalence of monopolistic competition or of oligopoly or of combinations of the two is recognized, many of the propositions which the Marshall-Wicksell generation of economists used to teach with the utmost confidence become either inapplicable or much more difficult to prove. This holds true, in the first place, of the propositions turning on the fundamental concept of equilibrium, i.e., a determinate state of the economic organism, toward which any given state of it is always gravitating and which displays certain simple properties. In the general case of oligopoly there is in fact no determinate equilibrium at all and the possibility presents itself that there may be an endless sequence of moves and countermoves, an indefinite state of warfare between firms. It is true that there are many special cases in which a state of equilibrium theoretically exists. In the second place, even in these cases not only is it much harder to attain than

[9] See, in particular, E. S. Chamberlin, *Theory of Monopolistic Competition*, and Joan Robinson, *The Economics of Imperfect Competition*.

the equilibrium in perfect competition, and still harder to preserve, but the "beneficial" competition of the classic type seems likely to be replaced by "predatory" or "cutthroat" competition or simply by struggles for control in the financial sphere. These things are so many sources of social waste, and there are many others such as the costs of advertising campaigns, the suppression of new methods of production (buying up of patents in order not to use them) and so on. And most important of all: under the conditions envisaged, equilibrium, even if eventually attained by an extremely costly method, no longer guarantees either full employment or maximum output in the sense of the theory of perfect competition. It *may* exist without full employment; it is *bound* to exist, so it seems, at a level of output below that maximum mark, because profit-conserving strategy, impossible in conditions of perfect competition, now not only becomes possible but imposes itself.

Well, does not this bear out what the man in the street (unless a businessman himself) always thought on the subject of private business? Has not modern analysis completely refuted the classical doctrine and justified the popular view? Is it not quite true after all, that there is little parallelism between producing for profit and producing for the consumer and that private enterprise is little more than a device to curtail production in order to extort profits which then are correctly described as tolls and ransoms?

III

THE PROCESS OF CREATIVE DESTRUCTION

THE theories of monopolistic and oligopolistic competition and
their popular variants may in two ways be made to serve the view
that capitalist reality is unfavorable to maximum performance in
production. One may hold that it always has been so and that all
along output has been expanding in spite of the secular sabotage
perpetrated by the managing bourgeoisie. Advocates of this proposition would have to produce evidence to the effect that the observed
rate of increase can be accounted for by a sequence of favorable circumstances unconnected with the mechanism of private enterprise
and strong enough to overcome the latter's resistance. This is precisely
the question which we shall discuss in Chapter V. However, those
who espouse this variant at least avoid the trouble about historical
fact that the advocates of the alternative proposition have to face.
This avers that capitalist reality once tended to favor maximum productive performance, or at all events productive performance so considerable as to constitute a major element in any serious appraisal of
the system; but that the later spread of monopolist structures, killing
competition, has by now reversed that tendency.

First, this involves the creation of an entirely imaginary golden age
of perfect competition that at some time somehow metamorphosed
itself into the monopolistic age, whereas it is quite clear that perfect
competition has at no time been more of a reality than it is at present.
Secondly, it is necessary to point out that the rate of increase in output
did not decrease from the nineties from which, I suppose, the prevalence of the largest-size concerns, at least in manufacturing industry,
would have to be dated; that there is nothing in the behavior of the
time series of total output to suggest a "break in trend"; and, most
important of all, that the modern standard of life of the masses
evolved during the period of relatively unfettered "big business." If
we list the items that enter the modern workman's budget and from
1899 on observe the course of their prices not in terms of money but
in terms of the hours of labor that will buy them—i.e., each year's
money prices divided by each year's hourly wage rates—we cannot fail
to be struck by the rate of the advance which, considering the spectacular improvement in qualities, seems to have been greater and not
smaller than it ever was before. If we economists were given less to
wishful thinking and more to the observation of facts, doubts would

immediately arise as to the realistic virtues of a theory that would have led us to expect a very different result. Nor is this all. As soon as we go into details and inquire into the individual items in which progress was most conspicuous, the trail leads not to the doors of those firms that work under conditions of comparatively free competition but precisely to the doors of the large concerns—which, as in the case of agricultural machinery, also account for much of the progress in the competitive sector—and a shocking suspicion dawns upon us that big business may have had more to do with creating that standard of life than with keeping it down.

The conclusions alluded to at the end of the preceding chapter are in fact almost completely false. Yet they follow from observations and theorems that are almost completely[1] true. Both economists and popular writers have once more run away with some fragments of reality they happened to grasp. These fragments themselves were mostly seen correctly. Their formal properties were mostly developed correctly. But no conclusions about capitalist reality as a whole follow from such fragmentary analyses. If we draw them nevertheless, we can be right only by accident. That has been done. And the lucky accident did not happen.

The essential point to grasp is that in dealing with capitalism we are dealing with an evolutionary process. It may seem strange that anyone can fail to see so obvious a fact which moreover was long ago emphasized by Karl Marx. Yet that fragmentary analysis which yields the bulk of our propositions about the functioning of modern capitalism persistently neglects it. Let us restate the point and see how it bears upon our problem.

Capitalism, then, is by nature a form or method of economic change and not only never is but never can be stationary. And this evolutionary character of the capitalist process is not merely due to the fact that economic life goes on in a social and natural environment which changes and by its change alters the data of economic action; this fact is important and these changes (wars, revolutions and so on) often condition industrial change, but they are not its prime movers. Nor is this evolutionary character due to a quasi-automatic increase in population and capital or to the vagaries of monetary systems of

---

[1] As a matter of fact, those observations and theorems are not completely satisfactory. The usual expositions of the doctrine of imperfect competition fail in particular to give due attention to the many and important cases in which, even as a matter of static theory, imperfect competition approximates the results of perfect competition. There are other cases in which it does not do this, but offers compensations which, while not entering any output index, yet contribute to what the output index is in the last resort intended to measure—the cases in which a firm defends its market by establishing a name for quality and service for instance. However, in order to simplify matters, we will not take issue with that doctrine on its own ground.

which exactly the same thing holds true. The fundamental impulse that sets and keeps the capitalist engine in motion comes from the new consumers' goods, the new methods of production or transportation, the new markets, the new forms of industrial organization that capitalist enterprise creates.

As we have seen in the preceding chapter, the contents of the laborer's budget, say from 1760 to 1940, did not simply grow on unchanging lines but they underwent a process of qualitative change. Similarly, the history of the productive apparatus of a typical farm, from the beginnings of the rationalization of crop rotation, plowing and fattening to the mechanized thing of today—linking up with elevators and railroads—is a history of revolutions. So is the history of the productive apparatus of the iron and steel industry from the charcoal furnace to our own type of furnace, or the history of the apparatus of power production from the overshot water wheel to the modern power plant, or the history of transportation from the mailcoach to the airplane. The opening up of new markets, foreign or domestic, and the organizational development from the craft shop and factory to such concerns as U. S. Steel illustrate the same process of industrial mutation—if I may use that biological term—that incessantly revolutionizes[2] the economic structure *from within*, incessantly destroying the old one, incessantly creating a new one. This process of Creative Destruction is the essential fact about capitalism. It is what capitalism consists in and what every capitalist concern has got to live in. This fact bears upon our problem in two ways.

First, since we are dealing with a process whose every element takes considerable time in revealing its true features and ultimate effects, there is no point in appraising the performance of that process *ex visu* of a given point of time; we must judge its performance over time, as it unfolds through decades or centuries. A system—any system, economic or other—that at *every* given point of time fully utilizes its possibilities to the best advantage may yet in the long run be inferior to a system that does so at *no* given point of time, because the latter's failure to do so may be a condition for the level or speed of long-run performance.

Second, since we are dealing with an organic process, analysis of what happens in any particular part of it—say, in an individual concern or industry—may indeed clarify details of mechanism but is inconclusive beyond that. Every piece of business strategy acquires its true significance only against the background of that process and

[2] Those revolutions are not strictly incessant; they occur in discrete rushes which are separated from each other by spans of comparative quiet. The process as a whole works incessantly however, in the sense that there always is either revolution or absorption of the results of revolution, both together forming what are known as business cycles.

within the situation created by it. It must be seen in its role in the perennial gale of creative destruction; it cannot be understood irrespective of it or, in fact, on the hypothesis that there is a perennial lull.

But economists who, *ex visu* of a point of time, look for example at the behavior of an oligopolist industry—an industry which consists of a few big firms—and observe the well-known moves and countermoves within it that seem to aim at nothing but high prices and restrictions of output are making precisely that hypothesis. They accept the data of the momentary situation as if there were no past or future to it and think that they have understood what there is to understand if they interpret the behavior of those firms by means of the principle of maximizing profits with reference to those data. The usual theorist's paper and the usual government commission's report practically never try to see that behavior, on the one hand, as a result of a piece of past history and, on the other hand, as an attempt to deal with a situation that is sure to change presently—as an attempt by those firms to keep on their feet, on ground that is slipping away from under them. In other words, the problem that is usually being visualized is how capitalism administers existing structures, whereas the relevant problem is how it creates and destroys them. As long as this is not recognized, the investigator does a meaningless job. As soon as it is recognized, his outlook on capitalist practice and its social results changes considerably.[3]

The first thing to go is the traditional conception of the *modus operandi* of competition. Economists are at long last emerging from the stage in which price competition was all they saw. As soon as quality competition and sales effort are admitted into the sacred precincts of theory, the price variable is ousted from its dominant position. However, it is still competition within a rigid pattern of invariant conditions, methods of production and forms of industrial organization in particular, that practically monopolizes attention. But in capitalist reality as distinguished from its textbook picture, it is not that kind of competition which counts but the competition from the new commodity, the new technology, the new source of supply, the new type of organization (the largest-scale unit of control for instance)—competition which commands a decisive cost or quality advantage and which strikes not at the margins of the profits and the outputs of the existing firms but at their foundations and their very lives. This kind of competition is as much more effective than the other as a bombardment is in comparison with forcing a door, and

[3] It should be understood that it is only our appraisal of economic performance and not our moral judgment that can be so changed. Owing to its autonomy, moral approval or disapproval is entirely independent of our appraisal of social (or any other) results, unless we happen to adopt a moral system such as utilitarianism which makes moral approval and disapproval turn on them *ex definitione*.

so much more important that it becomes a matter of comparative indifference whether competition in the ordinary sense functions more or less promptly; the powerful lever that in the long run expands output and brings down prices is in any case made of other stuff.

It is hardly necessary to point out that competition of the kind we now have in mind acts not only when in being but also when it is merely an ever-present threat. It disciplines before it attacks. The businessman feels himself to be in a competitive situation even if he is alone in his field or if, though not alone, he holds a position such that investigating government experts fail to see any effective competition between him and any other firms in the same or a neighboring field and in consequence conclude that his talk, under examination, about his competitive sorrows is all make-believe. In many cases, though not in all, this will in the long run enforce behavior very similar to the perfectly competitive pattern.

Many theorists take the opposite view which is best conveyed by an example. Let us assume that there is a certain number of retailers in a neighborhood who try to improve their relative position by service and "atmosphere" but avoid price competition and stick as to methods to the local tradition—a picture of stagnating routine. As others drift into the trade that quasi-equilibrium is indeed upset, but in a manner that does not benefit their customers. The economic space around each of the shops having been narrowed, their owners will no longer be able to make a living and they will try to mend the case by raising prices in tacit agreement. This will further reduce their sales and so, by successive pyramiding, a situation will evolve in which increasing potential supply will be attended by increasing instead of decreasing prices and by decreasing instead of increasing sales.

Such cases do occur, and it is right and proper to work them out. But as the practical instances usually given show, they are fringe-end cases to be found mainly in the sectors furthest removed from all that is most characteristic of capitalist activity.[4] Moreover, they are transient by nature. In the case of retail trade the competition that matters arises not from additional shops of the same type, but from the department store, the chain store, the mail-order house and the supermarket which are bound to destroy those pyramids sooner or later.[5]

4 This is also shown by a theorem we frequently meet with in expositions of the theory of imperfect competition, viz., the theorem that, under conditions of imperfect competition, producing or trading businesses tend to be irrationally small. Since imperfect competition is at the same time held to be an outstanding characteristic of modern industry we are set to wondering what world these theorists live in, unless, as stated above, fringe-end cases are all they have in mind.

5 The mere threat of their attack cannot, in the particular conditions, environmental and personal, of small-scale retail trade, have its usual disciplining influence, for the small man is too much hampered by his cost structure and, however

Now a theoretical construction which neglects this essential element of the case neglects all that is most typically capitalist about it; even if correct in logic as well as in fact, it is like *Hamlet* without the Danish prince.

---

well he may manage within his inescapable limitations, he can never adapt him self to the methods of competitors who can afford to sell at the price at which he buys.

IV

MONOPOLISTIC PRACTICES

WHAT has been said so far is really sufficient to enable the reader to deal with the large majority of the practical cases he is likely to meet and to realize the inadequacy of most of those criticisms of the profit economy which, directly or indirectly, rely on the absence of perfect competition. Since, however, the bearing of our argument on some of those criticisms may not be obvious at a glance, it will be worth our while to elaborate a little in order to make a few points more explicit.

1. We have just seen that, both as a fact and as a threat, the impact of new things—new technologies for instance—on the existing structure of an industry considerably reduces the long-run scope and importance of practices that aim, through restricting output, at conserving established positions and at maximizing the profits accruing from them. We must now recognize the further fact that restrictive practices of this kind, as far as they are effective, acquire a new significance in the perennial gale of creative destruction, a significance which they would not have in a stationary state or in a state of slow and balanced growth. In either of these cases restrictive strategy would produce no result other than an increase in profits at the expense of buyers except that, in the case of balanced advance, it might still prove to be the easiest and most effective way of collecting the means by which to finance additional investment.[1] But in the process of creative destruction, restrictive practices may do much to steady the ship and to alleviate temporary difficulties. This is in fact a very familiar argument which always turns up in times of depression and, as everyone knows, has become very popular with governments and their economic advisers—witness the NRA. While it has been so much misused and so faultily acted upon that most economists heartily despise it, those

---

[1] Theorists are apt to look upon anyone who admits this possibility as guilty of gross error, and to prove immediately that financing by borrowing from banks or from private savers or, in the case of public enterprise, financing from the proceeds of an income tax is much more rational than is financing from surplus profits collected through a restrictive policy. For some patterns of behavior they are quite right. For others they are quite wrong. I believe that both capitalism and communism of the Russian type belong in the latter category. But the point is that theoretical considerations, especially theoretical considerations of the short-run kind, cannot solve, although they contribute to the solution of, the problem which we shall meet again in the next part.

same advisers who are responsible for this[2] invariably fail to see its much more general rationale.

Practically any investment entails, as a necessary complement of entrepreneurial action, certain safeguarding activities such as insuring or hedging. Long-range investing under rapidly changing conditions, especially under conditions that change or may change at any moment under the impact of new commodities and technologies, is like shooting at a target that is not only indistinct but moving—and moving jerkily at that. Hence it becomes necessary to resort to such protecting devices as patents or temporary secrecy of processes or, in some cases, long-period contracts secured in advance. But these protecting devices which most economists accept as normal elements of rational management[3] are only special cases of a larger class comprising many others which most economists condemn although they do not differ fundamentally from the recognized ones.

If for instance a war risk is insurable, nobody objects to a firm's collecting the cost of this insurance from the buyers of its products. But that risk is no less an element in long-run costs, if there are no facilities for insuring against it, in which case a price strategy aiming at the same end will seem to involve unnecessary restriction and to be productive of excess profits. Similarly, if a patent cannot be secured or would not, if secured, effectively protect, other means may have to be used in order to justify the investment. Among them are a price policy that will make it possible to write off more quickly than would otherwise be rational, or additional investment in order to provide excess capacity to be used only for aggression or defense. Again, if long-period contracts cannot be entered into in advance, other means may have to be devised in order to tie prospective customers to the investing firm.

In analyzing such business strategy *ex visu* of a given point of time, the investigating economist or government agent sees price policies that seem to him predatory and restrictions of output that seem to him synonymous with loss of opportunities to produce. He does not see that restrictions of this type are, in the conditions of the perennial gale, incidents, often unavoidable incidents, of a long-run process of expansion which they protect rather than impede. There is no more of paradox in this than there is in saying that motorcars are traveling faster than they otherwise would *because* they are provided with brakes.

[2] In particular, it is easy to show that there is no sense, and plenty of harm, in a policy that aims at preserving "price parities."

[3] Some economists, however, consider that even those devices are obstructions to progress which, though perhaps necessary in capitalist society, would be absent in a socialist one. There is some truth in this. But that does not affect the proposition that the protection afforded by patents and so on is, in the conditions of a profit economy, on balance a propelling and not an inhibiting factor.

2. This stands out most clearly in the case of those sectors of the economy which at any time happen to embody the impact of new things and methods on the existing industrial structure. The best way of getting a vivid and realistic idea of industrial strategy is indeed to visualize the behavior of new concerns or industries that introduce new commodities or processes (such as the aluminum industry) or else reorganize a part or the whole of an industry (such as, for instance, the old Standard Oil Company).

As we have seen, such concerns are aggressors by nature and wield the really effective weapon of competition. Their intrusion can only in the rarest of cases fail to improve total output in quantity or quality, both through the new method itself—even if at no time used to full advantage—and through the pressure it exerts on the preexisting firms. But these aggressors are so circumstanced as to require, for purposes of attack and defense, also pieces of armor other than price and quality of their product which, moreover, must be strategically manipulated all along so that at any point of time they seem to be doing nothing but restricting their output and keeping prices high.

On the one hand, largest-scale plans could in many cases not materialize at all if it were not known from the outset that competition will be discouraged by heavy capital requirements or lack of experience, or that means are available to discourage or checkmate it so as to gain the time and space for further developments. Even the conquest of financial control over competing concerns in otherwise unassailable positions or the securing of advantages that run counter to the public's sense of fair play—railroad rebates—move, as far as long-run effects on total output alone are envisaged, into a different light;[4] they *may* be methods for removing obstacles that the institution of private property puts in the path of progress. In a socialist society that time and space would be no less necessary. They would have to be secured by order of the central authority.

On the other hand, enterprise would in most cases be impossible if

[4] The qualification added removes, I think, any just cause for offense that the above proposition might conceivably cause. In case that qualification is not explicit enough, I beg leave to repeat that the moral aspect is in this case, as it must be in every case, entirely unaffected by an economic argument. For the rest, let the reader reflect that even in dealing with indubitably criminal actions every civilized judge and every civilized jury take account of the ulterior purpose in pursuit of which a crime has occurred and of the difference it makes whether an action that is a crime has or has not also effects they consider socially desirable.

Another objection would be more to the point. If an enterprise can succeed only by such means, does not that prove in itself that it cannot spell social gain? A very simple argument can be framed in support of this view. But it is subject to a severe *ceteris paribus* proviso. That is to say, it holds for conditions which are just about equivalent to excluding the process of creative destruction—capitalist reality. On reflection, it will be seen that the analogy of the practices under discussion with patents is sufficient to show this.

it were not known from the outset that exceptionally favorable situations are likely to arise which if exploited by price, quality and quantity manipulation will produce profits adequate to tide over exceptionally unfavorable situations provided these are similarly managed Again this requires strategy that in the short run is often restrictive. In the majority of successful cases this strategy just manages to serve its purpose. In some cases, however, it is so successful as to yield profits far above what is necessary in order to induce the corresponding investment. These cases then provide the baits that lure capital on to untried trails. Their presence explains in part how it is possible for so large a section of the capitalist world to work for nothing: in the midst of the prosperous twenties just about half of the business corporations in the United States were run at a loss, at zero profits, or at profits which, if they had been foreseen, would have been inadequate to call forth the effort and expenditure involved.

Our argument however extends beyond the cases of new concerns, methods and industries. Old concerns and established industries, whether or not directly attacked, still live in the perennial gale. Situations emerge in the process of creative destruction in which many firms may have to perish that nevertheless would be able to live on vigorously and usefully if they could weather a particular storm. Short of such general crises or depressions, sectional situations arise in which the rapid change of data that is characteristic of that process so disorganizes an industry for the time being as to inflict functionless losses and to create avoidable unemployment. Finally, there is certainly no point in trying to conserve obsolescent industries indefinitely; but there is point in trying to avoid their coming down with a crash and in attempting to turn a rout, which may become a center of cumulative depressive effects, into orderly retreat. Correspondingly there is, in the case of industries that have sown their wild oats but are still gaining and not losing ground, such a thing as orderly advance.[5]

[5] A good example illustrative of this point—in fact of much of our general argument—is the postwar history of the automobile and the rayon industry. The first illustrates very well the nature and value of what we might call "edited" competition. The bonanza time was over by about 1916. A host of firms nevertheless crowded into the industry afterwards, most of which were eliminated by 1925. From a fierce life and death struggle three concerns emerged that by now account for over 80 per cent of total sales. They are under competitive pressure inasmuch as, in spite of the advantages of an established position, an elaborate sales and service organization and so on, any failure to keep up and improve the quality of their products or any attempt at monopolistic combination would call in new competitors. Among themselves, the three concerns behave in a way which should be called corespective rather than competitive: they refrain from certain aggressive devices (which, by the way, would also be absent in perfect competition); they keep up with each other and in doing so play for points at the frontiers. This has now gone on for upwards of fifteen years and it is not obvious that if conditions of theoretically perfect competition had prevailed during that period, better

All this is of course nothing but the tritest common sense. But it is being overlooked with a persistence so stubborn as sometimes to raise the question of sincerity. And it follows that, within the process of creative destruction, all the realities of which theorists are in the habit of relegating to books and courses on business cycles, there is another side to industrial self-organization than that which these theorists are contemplating. "Restraints of trade" of the cartel type as well as those which merely consist in tacit understandings about price competition may be effective remedies under conditions of depression. As far as they are, they may in the end produce not only steadier but also greater expansion of total output than could be secured by an entirely uncontrolled onward rush that cannot fail to be studded with catastrophes. Nor can it be argued that these catastrophes occur in any case. We know what has happened in each historical case. We have a very imperfect idea of what might have happened, considering the tremendous pace of the process, if such pegs had been entirely absent.

Even as now extended however, our argument does not cover all cases of restrictive or regulating strategy, many of which no doubt have that injurious effect on the long-run development of output which is uncritically attributed to all of them. And even in the cases our argument does cover, the net effect is a question of the circumstances and of the way in which and the degree to which industry regulates itself in each individual case. It is certainly as conceivable that an all-pervading cartel system might sabotage all progress as it is that it might realize, with smaller social and private costs, all that perfect competition is supposed to realize. This is why our argument does not amount to a case against state regulation. It does show that there is no general case for indiscriminate "trust-busting" or for the prosecution of everything that qualifies as a restraint of trade. Rational as distinguished from vindictive regulation by public authority turns out to be an extremely delicate problem which not every government agency, particularly when in full cry against big business, can be trusted to solve.[6] But our argument, framed to refute a preva-

---

or cheaper cars would now be offered to the public, or higher wages and more or steadier employment to the workmen. The rayon industry had its bonanza time in the twenties. It presents the features incident to introducing a commodity into fields fully occupied before and the policies that impose themselves in such conditions still more clearly than does the automobile industry. And there are a number of other differences. But fundamentally the case is similar. The expansion in quantity and quality of rayon output is common knowledge. Yet restrictive policy presided over this expansion at each individual point of time.

[6] Unfortunately, this statement is almost as effective a bar to agreement on policy as the most thoroughgoing denial of any case for government regulation could be. In fact it may embitter discussion. Politicians, public officers and economists can stand what I may politely term the whole-hog opposition of "economic royalists." Doubts about their competence, such as crowd upon us particularly when we see the legal mind at work, are much more difficult for them to stand.

lent *theory* and the inferences drawn therefrom about the relation between modern capitalism and the development of total output, only yields another *theory*, i.e., another outlook on facts and another principle by which to interpret them. For our purpose that is enough. For the rest, the facts themselves have the floor.

3. Next, a few words on the subject of Rigid Prices which has been receiving so much attention of late. It really is but a particular aspect of the problem we have been discussing. We shall define rigidity as follows: a price is rigid if it is less sensitive to changes in the conditions of demand and supply than it would be if perfect competition prevailed.[7]

Quantitatively, the extent to which prices are rigid in that sense depends on the material and the method of measurement we select and is hence a doubtful matter. But whatever the material or method, it is certain that prices are not nearly as rigid as they seem to be. There are many reasons why what in effect is a change in price should not show in the statistical picture; in other words, why there should be much spurious rigidity. I shall mention only one class of them which is closely connected with the facts stressed by our analysis.

I have adverted to the importance, for the capitalist process in general and for its competitive mechanism in particular, of the intrusion of new commodities. Now a new commodity may effectively bring down the preexisting structure and satisfy a given want at much lower prices per unit of service (transportation service for instance), and yet not a single recorded price need change in the process; flexibility in the relevant sense may be accompanied by rigidity in a formal sense. There are other cases, not of this type, in which price reduction is the sole motive for bringing out a new brand while the old one is left at the previous quotation—again a price reduction that does not show. Moreover, the great majority of new consumers' goods—particularly all the gadgets of modern life—are at first introduced in an experimental and unsatisfactory form in which they could never conquer their potential markets. Improvement in the quality of products is hence a practically universal feature of the development of individual concerns and of industries. Whether or not this improvement involves additional costs, a constant price per unit of an improving commodity should not be called rigid without further investigation. Of course, plenty of cases of genuine price rigidity remain—of

[7] This definition suffices for our purposes but would not be satisfactory for others. See D. D. Humphrey's article in the *Journal of Political Economy*, October 1937, and E. S. Mason's article in the *Review of Economic Statistics*, May 1938. Professor Mason has shown, among other things, that contrary to a widespread belief price rigidity is not increasing or, at all events, that it is no greater than it was forty years ago, a result which in itself suffices to invalidate some of the implications of the current doctrine of rigidity.

prices which are being kept constant as a matter of business policy or which remain unchanged because it is difficult to change, say, a price set by a cartel after laborious negotiations. In order to appraise the influence of this fact on the long-run development of output, it is first of all necessary to realize that this rigidity is essentially a short-run phenomenon. There are no major instances of long-run rigidity of prices. Whichever manufacturing industry or group of manufactured articles of any importance we choose to investigate over a period of time, we practically always find that in the long run prices do not fail to adapt themselves to technological progress—frequently they fall spectacularly in response to it[8]—unless prevented from doing so by monetary events and policies or, in some cases, by autonomous changes in wage rates which of course should be taken into account by appropriate corrections exactly as should changes in quality of products.[9] And our previous analysis shows sufficiently why in the process of capitalist evolution this must be so.

What the business strategy in question really aims at—all, in any case, that it can achieve—is to avoid seasonal, random and cyclical fluctuations in prices and to move only in response to the more fundamental changes in the conditions that underlie those fluctuations. Since these more fundamental changes take time in declaring themselves, this involves moving slowly by discrete steps—keeping to a price until new relatively durable contours have emerged into view. In technical language, this strategy aims at moving along a step function that will approximate trends. And that is what genuine and voluntary price rigidity in most cases amounts to. In fact, most economists do admit this, at least by implication. For though some of their arguments about rigidity would hold true only if the phenomenon were a long-run one—for instance most of the arguments averring that price rigidity keeps the fruits of technological progress from consumers—in practice they measure and discuss primarily cyclical rigidity and especially the fact that many prices do not, or do not promptly, fall in recessions and depressions. The real question is there-

[8] They do not as a rule fall as they would under conditions of perfect competition. But this is true only *ceteris paribus*, and this proviso robs the proposition of all practical importance. I have adverted to this point before and shall return to it below (§ 5).

[9] From a welfare standpoint, it is proper to adopt a definition different from ours, and to measure price changes in terms of the hours of labor that are currently necessary to earn the dollars which will buy given quantities of manufactured consumers' goods, taking account of changes of quality. We have already done this in the course of a previous argument. A long-run downward flexibility is then revealed that is truly impressive. Changes in price level raise another problem. So far as they reflect monetary influences they should be eliminated for most of the purposes of an investigation into rigidity. But so far as they reflect the combined effect of increasing efficiencies in all lines of production they should not.

fore how this short-run rigidity[10] may affect the long-run development of total output. Within this question, the only really important issue is this: prices that stay up in recession or depression no doubt influence the business situation in those phases of the cycles; if that influence is strongly injurious—making matters much worse than they would be with perfect flexibility all round—the destruction wrought each time might also affect output in the subsequent recoveries and prosperities and thus permanently reduce the rate of increase in total output below what it would be in the absence of those rigidities. Two arguments have been put forth in favor of this view.

In order to put the first into the strongest possible light, let us assume that an industry which refuses to reduce prices in recession goes on selling exactly the same quantity of product which it would sell if it had reduced them. Buyers are therefore out of pocket by the amount to which the industry profits from the rigidity. If these buyers are the kind of people who spend all they can and if the industry or those to whom its net returns go does not spend the increment it gets but either keeps it idle or repays bank loans, then total expenditure in the economy may be reduced thereby. If this happens, other industries or firms may suffer and if thereupon they restrict in turn, we may get a cumulation of depressive effects. In other words, rigidity may so influence the amount and distribution of national income as to decrease balances or to increase idle balances or, if we adopt a popular misnomer, savings. Such a case is conceivable. But the reader should have little difficulty in satisfying himself[11] that its practical importance, if any, is very small.

The second argument turns on the dislocating effects price rigidity may exert if, in the individual industry itself or elsewhere, it leads to an additional restriction of output, i.e., to a restriction greater than that which must in any case occur during depression. Since the most important conductor of those effects is the incident increase in unemployment—unstabilization of employment is in fact the indict-

---

[10] It should, however, be observed that this short run may last longer than the term "short run" usually implies—sometimes ten years and even longer. There is not one cycle, but there are many simultaneous ones of varying duration. One of the most important ones lasts on the average about nine years and a half. Structural changes requiring price adjustments do in important cases occur in periods of about that length. The full extent of the spectacular changes reveals itself only in periods much longer than this. To do justice to aluminum, rayon, or motorcar prices one must survey a period of about forty-five years.

[11] The best method of doing this is to work out carefully *all* the assumptions involved, not only in the strong case imagined but also in the weaker cases that are less unlikely to occur in practice. Moreover, it should not be forgotten that the profit due to keeping prices up may be the means of avoiding bankruptcy or at least the necessity of discontinuing operations, both of which might be much more effective in starting a downward "vicious spiral" than is a possible reduction in total expenditure. See the comments on the second argument.

ment most commonly directed against price rigidity—and the consequent decrease in total expenditure, this argument then follows in the tracks of the first one. Its practical weight is considerably reduced, although economists greatly differ as to the extent, by the consideration that in the most conspicuous cases price rigidity is motivated precisely by the low sensitiveness of demand to short-run price changes within the practicable range. People who in depression worry about their future are not likely to buy a new car even if the price were reduced by 25 per cent, especially if the purchase is easily postponable and if the reduction induces expectations of further reductions.

Quite irrespective of this however, the argument is inconclusive because it is again vitiated by a *ceteris paribus* clause that is inadmissible in dealing with our process of creative destruction. From the fact, so far as it is a fact, that at more flexible prices greater quantities could *ceteris paribus* be sold, it does not follow that either the output of the commodities in question, or total output and hence employment, would actually be greater. For inasmuch as we may assume that the refusal to lower prices strengthens the position of the industries which adopt that policy either by increasing their revenue or simply by avoiding chaos in their markets—that is to say, so far as this policy is something more than a mistake on their part—it may make fortresses out of what otherwise might be centers of devastation. As we have seen before, from a more general standpoint, total output and employment may well keep on a higher level with the restrictions incident to that policy than they would if depression were allowed to play havoc with the price structure.[12] In other words, under the conditions created by capitalist evolution, perfect and universal flexibility of prices might in depression further unstabilize the system, instead of stabilizing it as it no doubt would under the conditions envisaged by general theory. Again this is to a large extent recognized in those cases in which the economist is in sympathy with the interests immediately concerned, for instance in the case of labor and of agriculture; in those cases he admits readily enough that what looks like rigidity may be no more than regulated adaptation.

Perhaps the reader feels some surprise that so little remains of a doctrine of which so much has been made in the last few years. The rigidity of prices has become, with some people, the outstanding defect of the capitalist engine and—almost—the fundamental factor in the explanation of depressions. But there is nothing to wonder at in this. Individuals and groups snatch at anything that will qualify as a discovery lending support to the political tendencies of the hour. The

[12] The theorist's way to put the point is that in depression demand curves might shift downwards much more violently if all pegs were withdrawn from under all prices.

doctrine of price rigidity, with a modicum of truth to its credit, is not the worst case of this kind by a long way.

4. Another doctrine has crystallized into a slogan, viz., that in the era of big business the maintenance of the value of existing invest-ment—conservation of capital—becomes the chief aim of entrepre-neurial activity and bids fair to put a stop to all cost-reducing im-provement. Hence the capitalist order becomes incompatible with progress.

Progress entails, as we have seen, destruction of capital values in the strata with which the new commodity or method of production competes. In perfect competition the old investments must be adapted at a sacrifice or abandoned; but when there is no perfect competition and when each industrial field is controlled by a few big concerns, these can in various ways fight the threatening attack on their capital structure and try to avoid losses on their capital accounts; that is to say, they can and will fight progress itself.

So far as this doctrine merely formulates a particular aspect of re-strictive business strategy, there is no need to add anything to the argument already sketched in this chapter. Both as to the limits of that strategy and as to its functions in the process of creative destruction, we should only be repeating what has been said before. This becomes still more obvious if we observe that conserving capital values is the same thing as conserving profits. Modern theory tends in fact to use the concept Present Net Value of Assets (= capital values) in place of the concept of Profits. Both asset values and profits are of course not being simply conserved but maximized.

But the point about the sabotage of cost-reducing improvement still calls for comment in passing. As a little reflection will show, it is sufficient to consider the case of a concern that controls a technological device—some patent, say—the use of which would involve scrapping some or all of its plant and equipment. Will it, in order to conserve its capital values, refrain from using this device when a management not fettered by capitalist interests such as a socialist management could and would use it to the advantage of all?

Again it is tempting to raise the question of fact. The first thing a modern concern does as soon as it feels that it can afford it is to establish a research department every member of which knows that his bread and butter depends on his success in devising improvements. This practice does not obviously suggest aversion to technological progress. Nor can we in reply be referred to the cases in which patents acquired by business concerns have not been used promptly or not been used at all. For there may be perfectly good reasons for this; for example, the patented process may turn out to be no good or at least not to be in shape to warrant application on a commercial basis. Neither the inventors themselves nor the investigating economists or government officials are unbiased judges of this, and from their remonstrances or reports we may easily get a very distorted picture.[13]

But we are concerned with a question of theory. Everyone agrees that private and socialist managements will introduce improvements if, with the new method of production, the total cost per unit of product is expected to be smaller than the prime cost per unit of product with the method actually in use. If this condition is not fulfilled, then it is held that private management will not adopt a cost-reducing method until the existing plant and equipment is entirely written off, whereas socialist management would, to the social advantage, replace the old by any new cost-reducing method as soon as such a method becomes available, i.e., without regard to capital values. This however is not so.[14]

Private management, if actuated by the profit motive, cannot be interested in maintaining the values of any given building or machine any more than a socialist management would be. All that private management tries to do is to maximize the present net value of total assets which is equal to the discounted value of expected net returns. This amounts to saying that it will always adopt a new method of production which it believes will yield a larger stream of future income per unit of the corresponding stream of future outlay, both discounted to the present, than does the method actually in use. The value of past investment, whether or not paralleled by a bonded debt that has to be amortized, does not enter at all except in the sense and to the extent that it would also have to enter into the calculation underlying the decisions of a socialist management. So far as the use of the old machines saves future costs as compared with the immediate introduction of the new methods, the remainder of their service value is of course an element of the decision for both the capitalist and the socialist manager; otherwise bygones are bygones for both of them and any attempt to conserve the value of past investment would conflict as much with the rules following from the profit motive as it would conflict with the rules set for the behavior of the socialist manager.

[13] Incidentally, it should be noticed that the kind of restrictive practice under discussion, granted that it exists to a significant extent, would not be without compensatory effects on social welfare. In fact, the same critics who talk about sabotage of progress at the same time emphasize the *social* losses incident to the pace of capitalist progress, particularly the unemployment which that pace entails and which slower advance might mitigate to some extent. Well, is technological progress too quick or too slow for them? They had better make up their minds.

[14] It should be observed that even if the argument were correct, it would still be inadequate to support the thesis that capitalism is, under the conditions envisaged, "incompatible with technological progress." All that it would prove is, for some cases, the presence of a lag of ordinarily moderate length in the introduction of new methods.

It is however not true that private firms owning equipment the value of which is endangered by a new method which they also control—if they do not control it, there is no problem and no indictment —will adopt the new method only if total unit cost with it is smaller than prime unit cost with the old one, or if the old investment has been completely written off *according to the schedule decided on before the new method presented itself.* For if the new machines when installed are expected to outlive the rest of the period previously set for the use of the old machines, their discounted remainder value as of that date is another asset to be taken account of. Nor is it true, for analogous reasons, that a socialist management, if acting rationally, would always and immediately adopt any new method which promises to produce at smaller total unit costs or that this would be to the social advantage.

There is however another element[15] which profoundly affects behavior in this matter and which is being invariably overlooked. This is what might be called *ex ante* conservation of capital in expectation of further improvement. Frequently, if not in most cases, a going concern does not simply face the question whether or not to adopt a definite new method of production that is the best thing out and, in the form immediately available, can be expected to retain that position for some length of time. A new type of machine is in general but a link in a chain of improvements and may presently become obsolete. In a case like this it would obviously not be rational to follow the chain link by link regardless of the capital loss to be suffered each time. The real question then is at which link the concern should take action. The answer must be in the nature of a compromise between considerations that rest largely on guesses. But it will as a rule involve some waiting in order to see how the chain behaves. And to the outsider this may well look like trying to stifle improvement in order to conserve *existing* capital values. Yet even the most patient of comrades would revolt if a socialist management were so foolish as to follow the advice of the theorist and to keep on scrapping plant and equipment every year.

5. I have entitled this chapter as I did because most of it deals with the facts and problems that common parlance associates with monopoly or monopolistic practice. So far I have as much as possible refrained from using those terms in order to reserve for a separate section some comments on a few topics specifically connected with them. Nothing will be said however that we have not already met in one form or another.

(a) To begin with, there is the term itself. Monopolist means Single

---

[15] There are of course many other elements. The reader will please understand that in dealing with a few questions of principles it is impossible to do full justice to any of the topics touched upon.

Seller. Literally therefore anyone is a monopolist who sells anything that is not in every respect, wrapping and location and service included, exactly like what other people sell: every grocer, or every haberdasher, or every seller of "Good Humors" on a road that is not simply lined with sellers of the same brand of ice cream. This however is not what we mean when talking about monopolists. We mean only those single sellers whose markets are not open to the intrusion of would-be producers of the same commodity and of actual producers of similar ones or, speaking slightly more technically, only those single sellers who face a given demand schedule that is severely independent of their own action as well as of any reactions to their action by other concerns. The traditional Cournot-Marshall theory of monopoly as extended and amended by later authors holds only if we define it in this way and there is, so it seems, no point in calling anything a monopoly to which that theory does not apply.

But if accordingly we do define it like this, then it becomes evident immediately that pure cases of long-run monopoly must be of the rarest occurrence and that even tolerable approximations to the requirements of the concept must be still rarer than are cases of perfect competition. The power to exploit at pleasure a given pattern of demand—or one that changes independently of the monopolist's action and of the reactions it provokes—can under the conditions of intact capitalism hardly persist for a period long enough to matter for the analysis of total output, unless buttressed by public authority, for instance, in the case of fiscal monopolies. A modern business concern not *so* protected—i.e., even if protected by import duties or import prohibitions—and yet wielding that power (except temporarily) is not easy to find or even to imagine. Even railroads and power and light concerns had first to create the demand for their services and, when they had done so, to defend their market against competition. Outside the field of public utilities, the position of a single seller can in general be conquered—and retained for decades—only on the condition that he does not behave like a monopolist. Short-run monopoly will be touched upon presently.

Why then all this talk about monopoly? The answer is not without interest for the student of the psychology of political discussion. Of course, the concept of monopoly is being loosely used just like any other. People speak of a country's having a monopoly of something or other[16] even if the industry in question is highly competitive and so

[16] These so-called monopolies have of late come to the fore in connection with the proposal to withhold certain materials from aggressor nations. The lessons of this discussion have some bearing upon our problem by way of analogy. At first, much was thought of the possibilities of that weapon. Then, on looking more closely at it, people found their lists of such materials to be shrinking, because it became increasingly clear that there are very few things that cannot be either produced or substituted for in the areas in question. And finally a suspicion began

on. But this is not all. Economists, government agents, journalists and politicians in this country obviously love the word because it has come to be a term of opprobrium which is sure to rouse the public's hostility against any interest so labeled. In the Anglo-American world monopoly has been cursed and associated with functionless exploitation ever since, in the sixteenth and seventeenth centuries, it was English administrative practice to create monopoly positions in large numbers which, on the one hand, answered fairly well to the theoretical pattern of monopolist behavior and, on the other hand, fully justified the wave of indignation that impressed even the great Elizabeth.

Nothing is so retentive as a nation's memory. Our time offers other and more important instances of a nation's reaction to what happened centuries ago. That practice made the English-speaking public so monopoly-conscious that it acquired a habit of attributing to that sinister power practically everything it disliked about business. To the typical liberal bourgeòis in particular, monopoly became the father of almost all abuses—in fact, it became his pet bogey. Adam Smith,[17] thinking primarily of monopolies of the Tudor and Stuart type, frowned on them in awful dignity. Sir Robert Peel—who like most conservatives occasionally knew how to borrow from the arsenal of the demagogue—in his famous epilogue to his last period of office that gave so much offense to his associates, spoke of a monopoly of bread or wheat, though English grain production was of course perfectly competitive in spite of protection.[18] And in this country monopoly is being made practically synonymous with any large-scale business.

(b) The theory of simple and discriminating monopoly teaches that, excepting a limiting case, monopoly price is higher and monopoly output smaller than competitive price and competitive output. This is true provided that the method and organization of production—and everything else—are exactly the same in both cases. Actually how-

to dawn to the effect that even though some pressure can be exerted on them in the short run, long-run developments might eventually destroy practically all that was left on the lists.

[17] There was more excuse for that uncritical attitude in the case of Adam Smith and the classics in general than there is in the case of their successors because big business in our sense had not then emerged. But even so they went too far. In part this was due to the fact that they had no satisfactory theory of monopoly which induced them not only to apply the term rather promiscuously (Adam Smith and even Senior interpreted for instance the rent of land as a monopoly gain) but also to look upon the monopolists' power of exploitation as practically unlimited which is of course wrong even for the most extreme cases.

[18] This instance illustrates the way in which the term keeps on creeping into illegitimate uses. Protection of agriculture and a monopoly of agrarian products are entirely different things. The struggle was over protection and not over a non-existent cartel of either landowners or farmers. But in fighting protection it was just as well to beat up for applause. And there was evidently no simpler means of doing so than by calling protectionists monopolists.

ever there are superior methods available to the monopolist which either are not available at all to a crowd of competitors or are not available to them so readily: for there are advantages which, though not strictly unattainable on the competitive level of enterprise, are as a matter of fact secured only on the monopoly level, for instance, because monopolization may increase the sphere of influence of the better, and decrease the sphere of influence of the inferior, brains,[19] or because the monopoly enjoys a disproportionately higher financial standing. Whenever this is so, then that proposition is no longer true. In other words, this element of the case for competition may fail completely because monopoly prices are not necessarily higher or monopoly outputs smaller than competitive prices and outputs would be at the levels of productive and organizational efficiency that are within the reach of the type of firm compatible with the competitive hypothesis.

There cannot be any reasonable doubt that under the conditions of our epoch such superiority is as a matter of fact the outstanding feature of the typical large-scale unit of control, though mere size is neither necessary nor sufficient for it. These units not only arise in the process of creative destruction and function in a way entirely different from the static schema, but in many cases of decisive importance they provide the necessary form for the achievement. They largely create what they exploit. Hence the usual conclusion about their influence on long-run output would be invalid even if they were genuine monopolies in the technical sense of the term.

Motivation is quite immaterial. Even if the opportunity to set monopolist prices were the sole object, the pressure of the improved methods or of a huge apparatus would in general tend to shift the point of the monopolist's optimum toward or beyond the competitive cost price in the above sense, thus doing the work—partly, wholly, or more than wholly—of the competitive mechanism,[20] *even if re-*

---

[19] The reader should observe that while, as a broad rule, that particular type of superiority is simply indisputable, the inferior brains, especially if their owners are entirely eliminated, are not likely to admit it and that the public's and the recording economists' hearts go out to them and not to the others. This may have something to do with a tendency to discount the cost or quality advantages of quasi-monopolist combination that is at present as pronounced as was the exaggeration of them in the typical prospectus or announcement of sponsors of such combinations.

[20] The Aluminum Company of America is not a monopoly in the technical sense as defined above, among other reasons because it had to build up its demand schedule, which fact suffices to exclude a behavior conforming to the Cournot-Marshall schema. But most economists call it so and in the dearth of genuine cases we will for the purposes of this note do the same. From 1890 to 1929 the price of the basic product of this single seller fell to about 12 per cent or, correcting for the change in price level (B.L.S. index of wholesale prices), to about 8.8 per cent. Output rose from 30 metric tons to 103,400. Protection by patent ceased in 1909. Argument from costs and profits in criticism of this "monopoly" must

striction is practiced and excess capacity is in evidence all along. Of course if the methods of production, organization and so on are not improved by or in connection with monopolization as is the case with an ordinary cartel, the classical theorem about monopoly price and output comes into its own again.[21] So does another popular idea, viz., that monopolization has a soporific effect. For this, too, it is not difficult to find examples. But no general theory should be built upon it. For, especially in manufacturing industry, a monopoly position is in general no cushion to sleep on. As it can be gained, so it can be retained only by alertness and energy. What soporific influence there is in modern business is due to another cause that will be mentioned later.

(c) In the short run, genuine monopoly positions or positions approximating monopoly are much more frequent. The grocer in a village on the Ohio may be a true monopolist for hours or even days during an inundation. Every successful corner may spell monopoly for the moment. A firm specializing in paper labels for beer bottles may be so circumstanced—potential competitors realizing that what seem to be good profits would be immediately destroyed by their entering the field—that it can move at pleasure on a moderate but still finite stretch of the demand curve, at least until the metal label smashes that demand curve to pieces.

New methods of production or new commodities, especially the latter, do not *per se* confer monopoly, even if used or produced by a single firm. The product of the new method has to compete with the products of the old ones and the new commodity has to be introduced, i.e., its demand schedule has to be built up. As a rule neither patents nor monopolistic practices avail against that. But they may in cases of spectacular superiority of the new device, particularly if it can be leased like shoe machinery; or in cases of new commodities, the permanent demand schedule for which has been established before the patent has expired.

Thus it is true that there is or may be an element of genuine monopoly gain in those entrepreneurial profits which are the prizes offered by capitalist society to the successful innovator. But the quantitative importance of that element, its volatile nature and its function in the process in which it emerges put it in a class by itself. The main value to a concern of a single seller position that is secured by patent or monopolistic strategy does not consist so much in the opportunity

take it for granted that a multitude of competing firms would have been about equally successful in cost-reducing research, in the economical development of the productive apparatus, in teaching new uses for the product and in avoiding wasteful breakdowns. This is, in fact, being assumed by criticism of this kind; i.e., the propelling factor of modern capitalism is being assumed away.

[21] See however *supra,* § 1.

to behave temporarily according to the monopolist schema, as in the protection it affords against temporary disorganization of the market and the space it secures for long-range planning. Here however the argument merges into the analysis submitted before.

6. Glancing back we realize that most of the facts and arguments touched upon in this chapter tend to dim the halo that once surrounded perfect competition as much as they suggest a more favorable view of its alternative. I will now briefly restate our argument from this angle.

Traditional theory itself, even within its chosen precincts of a stationary or steadily growing economy, has since the time of Marshall and Edgeworth been discovering an increasing number of exceptions to the old propositions about perfect competition and, incidentally, free trade, that have shaken that unqualified belief in its virtues cherished by the generation which flourished between Ricardo and Marshall—roughly, J. S. Mill's generation in England and Francesco Ferrara's on the Continent. Especially the propositions that a perfectly competitive system is ideally economical of resources and allocates them in a way that is optimal with respect to a given distribution of income—propositions very relevant to the question of the behavior of output—cannot now be held with the old confidence.[22]

Much more serious is the breach made by more recent work in the field of dynamic theory (Frisch, Tinbergen, Roos, Hicks and others). Dynamic analysis is the analysis of sequences in time. In explaining why a certain economic quantity, for instance a price, is what we find it to be at a given moment, it takes into consideration not only the state of other economic quantities at the same moment, as static theory does, but also their state at preceding points of time, and the expectations about their future values. Now the first thing we discover in working out the propositions that thus relate quantities belonging to different points of time[23] is the fact that, once equilibrium has been destroyed by some disturbance, the process of establishing a new one is not so sure and prompt and economical as the old theory of perfect competition made it out to be; and the possibility that the very struggle for adjustment might lead such a system farther away from instead of nearer to a new equilibrium. This will happen in most cases unless the disturbance is small. In many cases, lagged adjustment is sufficient to produce this result.

All I can do here is to illustrate by the oldest, simplest and most familiar example. Suppose that demand and *intended* supply are in

[22] Since we cannot enter into the subject, I will refer the reader to Mr. R. F. Kahn's paper entitled "Some Notes on Ideal Output" (*Economic Journal* for March 1935), which covers much of this ground.

[23] The term dynamics is loosely used and carries many different meanings. The above definition was formulated by Ragnar Frisch.

equilibrium in a perfectly competitive market for wheat, but that bad weather reduces the crop below what farmers intended to supply. If price rises accordingly and the farmers thereupon produce that quantity of wheat which it would pay them to produce if that new price were the equilibrium price, then a slump in the wheat market will ensue in the following year. If now the farmers correspondingly restrict production, a price still higher than in the first year may result to induce a still greater expansion of production than occurred in the second year. And so on (as far as the pure logic of the process is concerned) indefinitely. The reader will readily perceive, from a survey of the assumptions involved, that no great fear need be entertained of ever higher prices' and ever greater outputs' alternating till doomsday. But even if reduced to its proper proportions, the phenomenon suffices to show up glaring weaknesses in the mechanism of perfect competition. As soon as this is realized much of the optimism that used to grace the practical implications of the theory of this mechanism passes out through the ivory gate.

But from our standpoint we must go further than that.[24] If we try to visualize how perfect competition works or would work in the process of creative destruction, we arrive at a still more discouraging result. This will not surprise us, considering that all the essential facts of that process are absent from the general schema of economic life that yields the traditional propositions about perfect competition. At the risk of repetition I will illustrate the point once more.

Perfect competition implies free entry into every industry. It is quite true, within that general theory, that free entry into all industries is a condition for optimal allocation of resources and hence for maximizing output. If our economic world consisted of a number of established industries producing familiar commodities by established and substantially invariant methods and if nothing happened except that additional men and additional savings combine in order to set up new firms of the existing type, then impediments to their entry into any industry they wish to enter would spell loss to the community. But perfectly free entry into a *new* field may make it impos-

---

[24] It should be observed that the defining feature of dynamic theory has nothing to do with the nature of the economic reality to which it is applied. It is a general method of analysis rather than a study of a particular process. We can use it in order to analyze a stationary economy, just as an evolving one can be analyzed by means of the methods of statics ("comparative statics"). Hence dynamic theory need not take, and as a matter of fact has not taken, any special cognizance of the process of creative destruction which we have taken to be the essence of capitalism. It is no doubt better equipped than is static theory to deal with many questions of mechanism that arise in the analysis of that process. But it is not an analysis of that process itself, and it treats the resulting individual disturbances of given states and structures just as it treats other disturbances. To judge the functioning of perfect competition from the standpoint of capitalist evolution is therefore not the same thing as judging it from the standpoint of dynamic theory.

sible to enter it at all. The introduction of new methods of production and new commodities is hardly conceivable with perfect—and perfectly prompt—competition from the start. And this means that the bulk of what we call economic progress is incompatible with it. As a matter of fact, perfect competition is and always has been temporarily suspended whenever anything new is being introduced—automatically or by measures devised for the purpose—even in otherwise perfectly competitive conditions.

Similarly, within the traditional system the usual indictment of rigid prices stands all right. Rigidity is a type of resistance to adaptation that perfect and prompt competition excludes. And for the kind of adaptation and for those conditions which have been treated by traditional theory, it is again quite true that such resistance spells loss and reduced output. But we have seen that in the spurts and vicissitudes of the process of creative destruction the opposite may be true: perfect and instantaneous flexibility may even produce functionless catastrophes. This of course can also be established by the general dynamic theory which, as mentioned above, shows that there are attempts at adaptation that intensify disequilibrium.

Again, under its own assumptions, traditional theory is correct in holding that profits above what is necessary in each individual case to call forth the equilibrium amount of means of production, entrepreneurial ability included, both indicate and in themselves imply net social loss and that business strategy that aims at keeping them alive is inimical to the growth of total output. Perfect competition would prevent or immediately eliminate such surplus profits and leave no room for that strategy. But since in the process of capitalist evolution these profits acquire new organic functions—I do not want to repeat what they are—that fact cannot any longer be unconditionally credited to the account of the perfectly competitive model, so far as the secular rate of increase in total output is concerned.

Finally, it can indeed be shown that, under the same assumptions which amount to excluding the most characteristic features of capitalist reality, a perfectly competitive economy is comparatively free from waste and in particular from those kinds of waste which we most readily associate with its counterpart. But this does not tell us anything about how its account looks under the conditions set by the process of creative destruction.

On the one hand, much of what without reference to those conditions would appear to be unrelieved waste ceases to qualify as such when duly related to them. The type of excess capacity for example that owes its existence to the practice of "building ahead of demand" or to the practice of providing capacity for the cyclical peaks of demand would in a regime of perfect competition be much reduced. But when *all* the facts of the case are taken into consideration, it is no longer correct to say that perfect competition wins out on that score. For though a concern that has to accept and cannot set prices would, in fact, use all of its capacity that can produce at marginal costs covered by the ruling prices, it does not follow that it would ever have the quantity and quality of capacity that big business has created and was able to create precisely because it is in a position to use it "strategically." Excess capacity of this type may—it does in some and does not in other cases—constitute a reason for claiming superiority for a socialist economy. But it should not without qualification be listed as a claim to superiority of the perfectly competitive species of capitalist economy as compared with the "monopoloid" species.

On the other hand, working in the conditions of capitalist evolution, the perfectly competitive arrangement displays wastes of its own. The firm of the type that is compatible with perfect competition is in many cases inferior in internal, especially technological, efficiency. If it is, then it wastes opportunities. It may also in its endeavors to improve its methods of production waste capital because it is in a less favorable position to evolve and to judge new possibilities. And, as we have seen before, a perfectly competitive industry is much more apt to be routed—and to scatter the bacilli of depression—under the impact of progress or of external disturbance than is big business. In the last resort, American agriculture, English coal mining, the English textile industry are costing consumers much more and are affecting *total* output much more injuriously than they would if controlled, each of them, by a dozen good brains.

Thus it is not sufficient to argue that because perfect competition is impossible under modern industrial conditions—or because it always has been impossible—the large-scale establishment or unit of control must be accepted as a necessary evil inseparable from the economic progress which it is prevented from sabotaging by the forces inherent in its productive apparatus. What we have got to accept is that it has come to be the most powerful engine of that progress and in particular of the long-run expansion of total output not only in spite of, but to a considerable extent through, this strategy which looks so restrictive when viewed in the individual case and from the individual point of time. In this respect, perfect competition is not only impossible but inferior, and has no title to being set up as a model of ideal efficiency. It is hence a mistake to base the theory of government regulation of industry on the principle that big business should be made to work as the respective industry would work in perfect competition. And socialists should rely for their criticisms on the virtues of a socialist economy rather than on those of the competitive model.

V

CLOSED SEASON

IT IS for the reader to decide how far the preceding analysis has attained its object. Economics is only an observational and interpretative science which implies that in questions like ours the room for difference of opinion can be narrowed but not reduced to zero. For the same reason the solution of our first problem only leads to the door of another which in an experimental science would not arise at all.

The first problem was to find out whether there is, as I have put it (p. 12), "an understandable relation" between the structural features of capitalism as depicted by various analytic "models" and the economic performance as depicted, for the epoch of intact or relatively unfettered capitalism, by the index of total output. My affirmative answer to this question was based upon an analysis that ran on lines approved by most economists up to the point at which what is usually referred to as the modern tendency toward monopolistic control entered the scene. After that my analysis deviated from the usual lines in an attempt to show that what practically everyone concedes to the capitalism of perfect competition (whether a theoretical construction, or, at some time or other, a historical reality) must also to even a greater degree be conceded to big-business capitalism. Since however we cannot put the driving power and the engine into an experiment station in order to let them perform under carefully controlled conditions, there is no way of proving, beyond the possibility of doubt, their adequacy to produce just that result, viz., the observed development of output. All we can say is that there was a rather striking performance and that the capitalist arrangement was favorable to producing it. And this is precisely why we cannot stop at our conclusion but have to face another problem.

A priori it might still be possible to account for the observed performance by exceptional circumstances which would have asserted themselves in any institutional pattern. The only way to deal with this possibility is to examine the economic and political history of the period in question and to discuss such exceptional circumstances as we may be able to find. We will attack the problem by considering those candidates for the role of exceptional circumstances not inherent in the business processes of capitalism which have been put up by economists or historians. There are five of them.

The first is government action which, though I quite agree with

Marx in holding that politics and policies are not independent factors but elements of the social process we are analyzing, may be considered as a factor external to the world of business for the purposes of this argument. The period from about 1870 to 1914 presents an almost ideal case. It would be difficult to find another equally free from either the stimuli or the depressants that may proceed from the political sector of the social process. The removal of the fetters from entrepreneurial activity and from industry and trade in general had largely been accomplished before. New and different fetters and burdens—social legislation and so on—were being imposed, but nobody will hold that they were major factors in the economic situation before 1914. There were wars. But none of them was economically important enough to exert vital effects one way or another. The Franco-German war that issued in the foundation of the German Empire might suggest a doubt. But the economically relevant event was after all the foundation of the Zollverein. There was armament expenditure. But in the circumstances of the decade ending in 1914 in which it assumed really important dimensions, it was a handicap rather than a stimulus.

The second candidate is gold. It is very fortunate that we need not enter into the thicket of questions that surrounds the *modus operandi* of the new plethora of gold which burst forth from about 1890 on. For since in the first twenty years of the period gold actually was scarce and since the rate of increase in total output was then no smaller than it was later on, gold production cannot have been a major factor in the productive performance of capitalism whatever it might have had to do with prosperities and depressions. The same holds true as regards monetary management which at that time was not of an aggressive but rather of an adaptive type.

Third, there was the increase in population which, whether a cause or a consequence of economic advance, certainly was one of the dominating factors in the economic situation. Unless we are prepared to aver that it was *wholly* consequential and to assume that any variation in output will always entail a corresponding variation in population while refusing to admit the converse nexus, all of which is of course absurd, that factor must be listed as an eligible candidate. For the moment, a brief remark will suffice to clarify the situation.

A greater number of gainfully employed people will in general produce more than a smaller number would whatever the social organization. Hence, if any part of the actual rate of increase in population during that epoch can be assumed—as of course it can—to have occurred independently of the results produced by the capitalist system in the sense that it would have occurred under any system, population must to that extent be listed as an external factor. To the same extent, the observed increase in total output does not measure, but exaggerates, capitalist performance.

Other things being equal, however, a greater number of gainfully employed people will in general produce less per head of employed or of population than a somewhat smaller number would whatever the social organization. This follows from the fact that the greater the number of workers, the smaller will be the amount of other factors with which the individual worker cooperates.[1] Hence, if output per head of population is chosen for measuring capitalist performance, then the observed increased is apt to understate the actual achievement, because part of this achievement has all along been absorbed in compensating for the fall in per capita output that would have occurred in its absence. Other aspects of the problem will be considered later on.

The fourth and fifth candidates command more support among economists but can easily be dismissed as long as we are dealing with past performance. The one is new land. The wide expanse of land that, economically speaking, entered the Americo-European sphere during that period; the huge mass of foodstuffs and raw materials, agricultural and other, that poured forth from it; all the cities and industries that everywhere grew up on the basis proffered by them— was this not a quite exceptional factor in the development of output, in fact a unique one? And was not this a boon that would have produced a vast access of wealth whatever the economic system it happened to impinge upon? There is a school of socialist thought that takes this view and in fact explains in this way the failure of Marx's predictions about ever-increasing misery to come true. The results of the exploitation of virgin environments they hold responsible for the fact that we did not see more of exploitation of labor; owing to that factor, the proletariat was permitted to enjoy a closed season.

There is no question about the importance of the opportunities afforded by the existence of new countries. And of course they were unique. But "objective opportunities"—that is to say, opportunities that exist independently of any social arrangement—are always prerequisites of progress, and each of them is historically unique. The presence of coal and iron ore in England or of petroleum in this and other countries is no less important and constitutes an opportunity that is no less unique. The whole capitalist process, like any other economic process that is evolutionary, consists in nothing else but exploiting such opportunities as they enter the businessman's horizon and there is no point in trying to single out the one under discussion in order to construe it as an external factor. There is less reason for doing so because the opening up of these new countries was achieved step by step through business enterprise and because business enter-

---

[1] This statement is far from satisfactory, but it seems to suffice for our purpose. The capitalist part of the world taken as a whole had by then certainly developed beyond the limits within which the opposite tendency is operative.

prise provided all the conditions for it (railroad and power plant construction, shipping, agricultural machinery and so on). Thus that
process was part and parcel of capitalist achievement and on a par
with the rest. Therefore the results rightfully enter our two per cent.
Again we might invoke the *Communist Manifesto* in support.

The last candidate is technological progress. Was not the observed
performance due to that stream of inventions that revolutionized the
technique of production rather than to the businessman's hunt for
profits? The answer is in the negative. The carrying into effect of those
technological novelties was of the essence of that hunt. And even the
inventing itself, as will be more fully explained in a moment, was
a function of the capitalist process which is responsible for the mental
habits that will produce invention. It is therefore quite wrong—and
also quite un-Marxian—to say, as so many economists do, that capitalist enterprise was one, and technological progress a second, distinct
factor in the observed development of output; they were essentially
one and the same thing or, as we may also put it, the former was the
propelling force of the latter.

Both the new land and the technological progress may become trou-
blesome as soon as we proceed to extrapolation. Though achievements
of capitalism, they may conceivably be achievements that cannot be
repeated. And though we now have established a reasonable case to the
effect that the observed behavior of output per head of population
during the period of full-fledged capitalism was not an accident but
may be held to measure roughly capitalist performance, we are faced
by still another question, viz., the question to what extent it is legiti-
mate to assume that the capitalist engine will—or would if allowed
to do so—work on in the near future, say for another forty years,
about as successfully as it did in the past.

VI

THE VANISHING OF INVESTMENT OPPORTUNITY

THE nature of this problem can be most tellingly displayed against the background of contemporaneous discussion. The present generation of economists has witnessed not only a world-wide depression of unusual severity and duration but also a subsequent period of halting and unsatisfactory recovery. I have already submitted my own interpretation[1] of these phenomena and stated the reasons why I do not think that they necessarily indicate a break in the trend of capitalist evolution. But it is natural that many if not most of my fellow economists should take a different view. As a matter of fact they feel, exactly as some of their predecessors felt between 1873 and 1896—though then this opinion was mainly confined to Europe—that a fundamental change is upon the capitalist process. According to this view, we have been witnessing not merely a depression and a bad recovery, accentuated perhaps by anti-capitalist policies, but the symptoms of a permanent loss of vitality which must be expected to go on and to supply the dominating theme for the remaining movements of the capitalist symphony; hence no inference as to the future can be drawn from the functioning of the capitalist engine and of its performance in the past.

This view is being held by many with whom the wish is not father to the thought. But we shall understand why socialists with whom it is, should have with particular alacrity availed themselves of the windfall—some of them to the point of shifting the base of their anti-capitalist argument completely to this ground. In doing so, they reaped the additional advantage of being able to fall back once more upon Marxian tradition which, as I have pointed out before, the trained economists among them had felt compelled to discard more and more. For, in the sense explained in the first chapter, Marx had predicted such a state of things: according to him capitalism, before actually breaking down, would enter into a stage of permanent crisis, temporarily interrupted by feeble upswings or by favorable chance occurrences. Nor is this all. One way of putting the matter from a Marxian standpoint is to stress the effects of capital accumulation and capital agglomeration on the rate of profits and, through the rate of profits, on the opportunity to invest. Since the capitalist process always

---

[1] See ch. I, p. 4.

has been geared to a large amount of current investment, even partial elimination of it would suffice to make plausible the forecast that the process is going to flop. This particular line in the Marxist argument no doubt seems to agree well not only with some outstanding facts of the past decade—unemployment, excess reserves, gluts in money markets, unsatisfactory margins of profits, stagnation of private investment—but also with several non-Marxist interpretations. There is surely no such gulf between Marx and Keynes as there was between Marx and Marshall or Wicksell. Both the Marxist doctrine and its non-Marxist counterpart are well expressed by the self-explanatory phrase that we shall use: the theory of vanishing investment opportunity.[2]

It should be observed that this theory really raises three distinct problems. The first is akin to the question that heads this part. Since nothing in the social world can ever be *aere perennius* and since the capitalist order is essentially the framework of a process not only of economic but also of social change, there is not much room for difference about the answer. The second question is whether the forces and mechanisms offered by the theory of vanishing investment opportunity are the ones to stress. In the following chapters I am going to submit another theory of what will eventually kill capitalism, but a number of parallelisms will remain. There is however a third problem. Even if the forces and mechanisms stressed by the theory of vanishing investment opportunity were in themselves adequate to establish the presence in the capitalist process of a long-run tendency toward ultimate deadlock, it does not necessarily follow that the vicissitudes of the past decade have been due to them and—which it is important to add for our purpose—that similar vicissitudes should therefore have to be expected to persist for the next forty years.

For the moment we are mainly concerned with the third problem. But much of what I am going to say also bears on the second. The factors that are held to justify a pessimistic forecast concerning the performance of capitalism in the near future and to negative the idea that past performance may be repeated may be divided into three groups.

There are, first, the environmental factors. It has been stated and will have to be established that the capitalist process produces a distribution of political power and a socio-psychological attitude—expressing itself in corresponding policies—that are hostile to it and may be expected to gather force so that they will eventually prevent the capitalist engine from functioning. This phenomenon I will set aside for later consideration. What follows now must be read with the appropriate proviso. But it should be noted that that attitude and cognate factors also affect the motive power of the bourgeois profit

---

[2] See my *Business Cycles*, ch. xv.

economy itself, and that hence the proviso covers more than one might think at first sight—more, at any rate, than mere "politics."

Then there is the capitalist engine itself. The theory of vanishing investment opportunity does not necessarily include, but as a matter of fact is apt to be in alliance with, the other theory that modern largest-scale business represents a petrified form of capitalism in which restrictive practices, price rigidities, exclusive attention to the conservation of existing capital values and so on are naturally inherent. This has been dealt with already.

Finally, there is what may be described as the "material" the capitalist engine feeds on, i.e., the opportunities open to new enterprise and investment. The theory under discussion puts so much emphasis on this element as to justify the label we have affixed to it. The main reasons for holding that opportunities for private enterprise and investment are vanishing are these: saturation, population, new lands, technological possibilities, and the circumstance that many existing investment opportunities belong to the sphere of public rather than of private investment.

1. For every given state of human wants and of technology (in the widest possible sense of the term) there is of course for every rate of real wages a definite amount of fixed and circulating capital that will spell saturation. If wants and methods of production had been frozen for good at their state in 1800, such a point would have been reached long ago. But is it not conceivable that wants may some day be so completely satisfied as to become frozen forever after? Some implications of this case will presently be developed, but so long as we deal with what may happen during the next forty years we evidently need not trouble ourselves about this possibility.

If ever it should materialize, then the current decline in birth rate, still more an actual fall in population, would indeed become an important factor in reducing opportunities for investment other than replacement. For if everyone's wants were satisfied or nearly satisfied, increase in the number of consumers would *ex hypothesi* be the only major source of additional demand. But independently of that possibility, decrease in the rate of increase in population does not *per se* endanger investment opportunity or the rate of increase in total output per head.[3] Of this we can easily satisfy ourselves by a brief examination of the usual argument to the contrary.

[3] This also holds true for a small decline in absolute numbers of people such as may occur in Great Britain before very long (see E. Charles, *London and Cambridge Economic Service*, Memo. No. 40). A considerable absolute decline would raise additional problems. These we shall neglect however because this cannot be expected to occur during the space of time under consideration. Still other problems, economic as well as political and socio-psychological, are presented by the aging of a population. Though they are beginning to assert themselves already—there is practically such a thing as a "lobby of the old"—we cannot enter into

On the one hand it is being held that a declining rate of increase in total population *ipso facto* spells a declining rate of increase in output and hence of investment because it restricts the expansion of demand. This does not follow. Want and effective demand are not the same thing. If they were, the poorest nations would be the ones to display the most vigorous demand. As it is, the income elements set free by the falling birth rate may be diverted to other channels and they are particularly apt to be so diverted in all those cases in which the desire to expand alternative demands is the very motive of child-lessness. A modest argument can indeed be made out by stressing the fact that the lines of demand characteristic of an increasing population are particularly calculable and thus afford particularly reliable invest-ment opportunities. But the desires that provide alternative oppor-tunities are, in the given state of satisfaction of wants, not much less so. Of course the prognosis for certain individual branches of produc-tion, especially for agriculture, is in fact not a bright one. But this must not be confused with the prognosis for total output.[4]

On the other hand, we might argue that the declining rate of increase in population will tend to restrict output from the supply side. Rapid increase was in the past frequently one of the conditions of the observed development of output, and we might conclude *a contrario* that increasing scarcity of the labor factor might be expected to be a limiting factor. However, we do not hear much of this argu-ment and for very good reasons. The observation that at the begin-ning of 1940 output of manufacturing industry in the United States was about 120 per cent of the average for 1923-1925 whereas factory employment was at about 100 per cent supplies an answer that is adequate for the calculable future. The extent of current unemploy-ment; the fact that with a falling birth rate women are increasingly set free for productive work and that the falling death rate means prolongation of the useful period of life; the unexhausted stream of labor-saving devices; the possibility, increasing relatively to what it would be in the case of rapid increase of population, of avoiding complementary factors of production of inferior quality (warding off in part the operation of the law of diminishing-returns)—all this gives

---

them either. But it should be observed that, as long as retiring ages remain the same, the percentage share of those who have to be provided for without con-tributing need not be affected by a decreasing percentage of persons under fifteen.

[4] There seems to be an impression, prevalent with many economists, to the effect that an increase in population *per se* provides another source of demand for investment. Why—must not all these new workmen be equipped with tools and their complement of raw material? This however is by no means obvious. Unless the increase is allowed to depress wages, the implication as to investment oppor-tunity lacks motivation, and even in that case reduction of investment per head employed would have to be expected.

ample support to Mr. Colin Clark's expectation that product per man-hour is going to rise during the next generation.[5]

Of course, the labor factor may be made artificially scarce through high-wage and short-hour policies and through political interference with the discipline of the labor force. Comparison of the economic performance in the United States and France from 1933 to 1940 with the economic performance of Japan and Germany during the same years suggests in fact that something of this kind has already occurred. But this belongs to the group of environmental factors.

As my argument will abundantly show before long, I am very far indeed from making light of the phenomenon under discussion. The falling birth rate seems to me to be one of the most significant features of our time. We shall see that even from a purely economic standpoint it is of cardinal importance, both as a symptom and as a cause of changing motivation. This however is a more complicated matter. Here we are concerned only with the mechanical effects of a decreasing rate of increase in population and these certainly do not support any pessimistic forecast as to the development of output per head during the next forty years. As far as that goes, those economists who predict a "flop" on this ground simply do what unfortunately economists have always been prone to do: as once they worried the public, on quite inadequate grounds, with the economic dangers of excessive numbers of mouths to feed,[6] so they worry it now, on no better grounds, with the economic dangers of deficiencies.

2. Next as to the opening up of new lands—that unique opportunity for investment which cannot ever recur. Even if, for the sake of argument, we grant that humanity's geographical frontier is closed for good—which is not in itself very obvious in view of the fact that at present there are deserts where once there were fields and populous cities—and even if we further grant that nothing will ever contribute to human *welfare* as much as did the foodstuffs and raw materials from those new lands—which is more plausible—it does not follow that total output per head must therefore decline, or increase at a smaller rate, during the next half-century. This would indeed have to be expected if the lands that in the nineteenth century entered the capitalist sphere had been exploited in the sense that diminishing

[5] *National Income and Outlay*, p. 21.

[6] Forecasts of future populations, from those of the seventeenth century on, were practically always wrong. For this, however, there is some excuse. There may be even for Malthus's doctrine. But I cannot see any excuse for its survival. In the second half of the nineteenth century it should have been clear to anyone that the only valuable things about Malthus's law of population are its qualifications. The first decade of this century definitely showed that it was a bogey. But no less an authority than Mr. Keynes attempted to revitalise it in the post-war period! And as late as 1925, Mr. H. Wright in his book on Population spoke of "wasting the gains of civilization on a mere increase in numbers." Will economics never come of age?

returns would now be due to assert themselves. This however is not the case and, as was just pointed out, the decreasing rate of increase in population removes from the range of practical considerations the idea that nature's response to human effort either already is or must soon become less generous than it has been. Technological progress effectively turned the tables on any such tendency, and it is one of the safest predictions that in the calculable future we shall live in an *embarras de richesse* of both foodstuffs and raw materials, giving all the rein to expansion of total output that we shall know what to do with. This applies to mineral resources as well.

There remains another possibility. Though the current output per head of foodstuffs and raw materials need not suffer and may even increase, the vast opportunities for enterprise and hence for investment that were afforded by the task of developing the new countries seem to have vanished with its completion and all sorts of difficulties are being predicted from the resulting reduction of outlets for savings. We will assume again for the sake of argument that those countries actually are developed for good and that savings, failing to adapt themselves to a reduction of outlets, might cause troubles and wastes unless other outlets open up instead. Both assumptions are indeed most unrealistic. But there is no necessity for us to question them because the conclusion as to the future development of output is contingent upon a third one that is completely gratuitous, viz., the absence of other outlets.

This third assumption is simply due to lack of imagination and exemplifies a mistake that very frequently distorts historical interpretation. The particular features of a historic process that impress the analyst tend in his mind to slip into the position of fundamental causes whether they have a claim to that role or not. For instance, what is usually referred to as the Rise of Capitalism roughly coincides with the influx of silver from the Potosí mines and with a political situation in which the expenditure of princes habitually outran their revenue so that they had to borrow incessantly. Both facts are obviously relevant in a variety of ways to the economic developments of those times—even peasants' revolts and religious upheavals may without absurdity be linked up with them. The analyst thereupon is apt to jump to the conclusion that the rise of the capitalist order of things is causally connected with them in the sense that without them (and a few other factors of the same type) the feudal world would have failed to transform itself into the capitalist one. But this is really another proposition and one for which there is, on the face of it, no warrant whatsoever. All that can be averred is that this was the road by which events traveled. It does not follow that there was no other. In this case, by the way, it cannot even be held that those factors favored capitalist development for though they certainly did do so in some respects they obviously retarded it in others.

Similarly, as we have seen in the preceding chapter, the opportunities for enterprise afforded by the new areas to be exploited were certainly unique, but only in the sense in which all opportunities are. It is gratuitous to assume not only that the "closing of the frontier" will cause a vacuum but also that whatever steps into the vacant place must necessarily be less important in any of the senses we may choose to give to that word. The conquest of the air may well be more important than the conquest of India was—we must not confuse geographical frontiers with economic ones.

It is true that the relative positions of countries or regions may significantly change as one type of investment opportunity is replaced by another. The smaller a country or region is and the more closely its fortunes are wedded to one particular element in the productive process, the less confidence we shall feel as to the future in store for it when that element is played out. Thus agricultural countries or regions *may* lose permanently by the competitive synthetic products (rayon, dyes, synthetic rubber for instance), and it may be no comfort to them that, if the process be taken as a whole, there may be net gain in total output. It is also true that the possible consequences of this may be much intensified by the division of the economic world into hostile national spheres. And it is finally true that all we can assert is that the vanishing of the investment opportunities incident to the development of new countries—if they are already vanishing—*need* not cause a void that would necessarily affect the rate of increase in total output. We cannot assert that they actually will be replaced by at least equivalent ones. We may point to the fact that from that development further developments naturally arise in those same countries or in others; we may put some trust in the ability of the capitalist engine to find or create ever new opportunities since it is geared to this very purpose; but such considerations do not carry us beyond our negative result. And recalling our reasons for embarking upon the subject, this is quite enough.

3. An analogous argument applies to the widely accepted view that the great stride in technological advance has been made and that but minor achievements remain. So far as this view does not merely render the impressions conceived from the state of things during and after the world crisis—when an apparent absence of novel propositions of the first magnitude was part of the familiar pattern of any great depression—it exemplifies still better than did the "closing of humanity's frontier" that error in interpretation economists are so prone to commit. We are just now in the downgrade of a wave of enterprise that created the electrical power plant, the electrical industry, the electrified farm and home and the motorcar. We find all that

very marvelous, and we cannot for our lives see where opportunities of comparable importance are to come from. As a matter of fact however, the promise held out by the chemical industry alone is much greater than what it was possible to anticipate in, say, 1880, not to mention the fact that the mere utilization of the achievement of the age of electricity and the production of modern homes for the masses would suffice to provide investment opportunities for quite a time to come.

Technological possibilities are an uncharted sea. We may survey a geographical region and appraise, though only with reference to a given technique of agricultural production, the relative fertility of individual plots. Given that technique and disregarding its possible future developments, we may then imagine (though this would be wrong historically) that the best plots are first taken into cultivation, after them the next best ones and so on. At any given time during this process it is only relatively inferior plots that remain to be exploited in the future. But we cannot reason in this fashion about the future possibilities of technological advance. From the fact that some of them have been exploited before others, it cannot be inferred that the former were more productive than the latter. And those that are still in the lap of the gods may be more or less productive than any that have thus far come within our range of observation. Again this yields only a negative result which even the fact that technological "progress" tends, through systemization and rationalization of research and of management, to become more effective and sure-footed, is powerless to turn into a positive one. But for us the negative result suffices: there is no reason to expect slackening of the rate of output through exhaustion of technological possibilities.

4. Two variants of this branch of the theory of vanishing investment opportunity remain to be noticed. Some economists have held that the labor force of every country had to be fitted out at some time or other with the necessary equipment. This, so they argue, has been accomplished roughly in the course of the nineteenth century. While it was being accomplished, it incessantly created new demand for capital goods, whereas, barring additions, only replacement demand remains forever after. The period of capitalist armament thus would turn out to be a unique intermezzo after all, characterized by the capitalist economy's straining every nerve in order to create for itself the necessary complement of tools and machines, and thus becoming equipped for the purpose of producing for further production at a rate which it is now impossible to keep up. This is a truly astounding picture of the economic process. Was there no equipment in the eighteenth century or, in fact, at the time our ancestors dwelled in caves? And if there was, why should the additions that occurred in the nineteenth century have been more saturating than any that went before? Moreover, additions to the armor of capitalism are as a rule competitive

with the preexisting pieces of it. They destroy the economic usefulness of the latter. Hence the task of providing equipment can never be solved once for all. The cases in which replacement reserves are adequate to solve it—as they normally would be in the absence of technological change—are exceptions. This is particularly clear where the new methods of production are embodied in new industries; obviously the automobile plants were not financed from the depreciation accounts of railroads.

The reader will no doubt observe that even if we were able to accept the premises of this argument, no pessimistic forecast about the rate of expansion of total output would necessarily follow. On the contrary he might draw the opposite inference, viz., that the possession of an extensive stock of capital goods that acquires economic immortality through continuous renewal should if anything facilitate further increase in total output. If so, he is quite right. The argument rests entirely on the disturbance to be expected if an economy geared to capital production faces a reduced rate of increase in the corresponding demand. But this disturbance which is not of sudden occurrence can easily be exaggerated. The steel industry for instance has not experienced great difficulties in transforming itself from an industry that produced capital goods almost exclusively into one that produces primarily durable consumers' goods or semi-finished products for the production of durable consumers' goods. And though compensation may not be possible within each existing capital goods industry, the principle involved is the same in all cases.

The other variant is this. The great bursts of economic activity that used to spread the symptoms of prosperity all over the economic organism have of course always been associated with expansions of producers' expenditure that were in turn associated with the construction of additional plant and equipment. Now some economists have discovered, or think they have discovered, that at the present time new technological processes tend to require less fixed capital in this sense than they used to in the past, particularly in the epoch of railroad building. The inference is that spending for capital construction will henceforth decrease in relative importance. Since this will adversely affect those intermittent bursts of economic activity that evidently have much to do with the observed rate of increase in total output, it further follows that this rate is bound to decline, especially if saving goes on at the old rate.

This tendency of new technological methods to become increasingly capital-saving has not so far been adequately established. Statistical evidence up to 1929—later data do not qualify for the purpose—point the other way. All that the sponsors of the theory in question have offered is a number of isolated instances to which it is possible to oppose others. But let us grant that such a tendency exists. We have then the same formal problem before us which exercised so many

economists of the past in the case of labor-saving devices. These may
affect the interests of labor favorably or adversely, but nobody doubts
that on the whole they are favorable to an expansion of output. And
this is—barring possible disturbances in the saving-investment process
which it is the fashion to exaggerate—no different in the case of devices
that economize outlay on capital goods *per unit of the final product.*
In fact, it is not far from the truth to say that almost any new process
that is economically workable economizes both labor and capital.
Railroads were presumably capital-saving as compared with the outlay
that transportation, by mailcoach or cart, of the same numbers of
passengers and of the same quantities of goods that actually are being
transported by railroads now would have involved. Similarly silk
production by mulberry trees and silkworms may be more capital-
consuming—I don't know—than the production of an equivalent
amount of rayon fabric would be. That may be very sad for the
owners of capital already sunk in the former. But it need not even
mean decrease of investment opportunity. It certainly does not necessarily mean decrease in the expansion of output. Those who hope to
see capitalism break down solely by virtue of the fact that the unit of
capital goes further in productive effect than it used to, may have to
wait long indeed.

5. Finally, since the subject is usually dealt with by economists who
aim at impressing upon the public the necessity of governmental
deficit spending, another point never fails to turn up, viz., that such
opportunities for investment as remain are more suited for public
than they are for private enterprise. This is true to some extent. First,
with increasing wealth certain lines of expenditure are likely to gain
ground which do not naturally enter into any cost-profit calculation,
such as expenditure on the beautification of cities, on public health
and so on. Second, an ever-widening sector of industrial activity tends
to enter the sphere of public management, such as means of communication, docks, power production, insurance and so on, simply
because these industries become increasingly amenable to the methods
of public administration. National and municipal investment could
thus be expected to expand, absolutely and relatively, even in a thoroughly capitalist society, just as other forms of public planning would.

But that is all. In order to recognize it we need not make any hypothesis about the course of things in the private sector of industrial
activity. Moreover, for the purpose in hand it is immaterial whether
in the future investment and the incident expansion of output will
to a greater or a lesser extent be financed and managed by public
rather than by private agencies unless it be held in addition that
public financing will impose itself because private business would
not be able to face the deficits to be expected in the future from *any*
investment. This however has been dealt with before.

VII

THE CIVILIZATION OF CAPITALISM

LEAVING the precincts of purely economic considerations, we now turn to the cultural complement of the capitalist economy—to its socio-psychological *superstructure*, if we wish to speak the Marxian language—and to the mentality that is characteristic of capitalist society and in particular of the bourgeois class. In desperate brevity, the salient facts may be conveyed as follows.

Fifty thousand years ago man confronted the dangers and opportunities of his environment in a way which some "prehistorians," sociologists and ethnologists agree was roughly equivalent to the attitude of modern primitives.[1] Two elements of this attitude are particularly important for us: the "collective" and "affective" nature of the primitive mental process and, partly overlapping, the role of what, not quite correctly, I shall here call magic. By the first I designate the fact that in small and undifferentiated or not much differentiated social groups collective ideas impose themselves much more stringently on the individual mind than they do in big and complex groups; and that conclusions and decisions are arrived at by methods which for our purpose may be characterized by a negative criterion: the disregard of what we call logic and, in particular, of the rule that excludes contradiction. By the second I designate the use of a set of beliefs which are not indeed completely divorced from experience—no magic device *Affective* can survive an unbroken sequence of failures—but which insert, into the sequence of observed phenomena, entities or influences derived from non-empirical sources.[2] The similarity of this type of mental

---

[1] Research of this type goes far back. But I believe that a new stage of it ought to be dated from the works of Lucien Lévy-Bruhl. See in particular his *Fonctions mentales dans les sociétés inférieures* (1909) and *Le surnaturel et la nature dans la mentalité primitive* (1931). There is a long way between the position held in the first and the position held in the second work, the milestones of which are discernible in *Mentalité primitive* (1921) and *L'ame primitive* (1927). For us, Lévy-Bruhl is a particularly useful authority because he fully shares our thesis—in fact his work starts from it—that the "executive" functions of thinking and the mental structure of man are determined, partly at least, by the structure of the society within which they develop. It is immaterial that, with Lévy-Bruhl, this principle hails not from Marx but from Comte.

[2] A friendly critic of the above passage expostulated with me on the ground that I could not possibly mean what it says because in that case I should have to call the physicist's "force" a magic device. That is precisely what I do mean, unless it is agreed that the term Force is merely a name for a constant times the second time derivative of displacement. See the next but one sentence in the text.

process with the mental processes of neurotics has been pointed out by G. Dromard (1911; his term, *délire d'interprétation,* is particularly suggestive) and S. Freud (*Totem und Tabu,* 1913). But it does not follow that it is foreign to the mind of normal man of our own time. On the contrary, any discussion of political issues may convince the reader that a large and—for action—most important body of our own processes is of exactly the same nature.

Rational thought or behavior and a rationalistic civilization therefore do not imply absence of the criteria mentioned but only a slow though incessant widening of the sector of social life within which individuals or groups go about dealing with a given situation, first, by trying to make the best of it more or less—never wholly—according to their own lights; second, by doing so according to those rules of consistency which we call logic; and third, by doing so on assumptions which satisfy two conditions: that their number be a minimum and that every one of them be amenable to expression in terms of potential experience.[3]

All this is very inadequate of course but it suffices for our purpose. There is however one more point about the concept of rationalist civilizations that I will mention here for future reference. When the habit of rational analysis of, and rational behavior in, the daily tasks of life has gone far enough, it turns back upon the mass of collective ideas and criticizes and to some extent "rationalizes" them by way of such questions as why there should be kings and popes or subordination or tithes or property. Incidentally, it is important to notice that, while most of us would accept such an attitude as the symptom of a "higher stage" of mental development, this value judgment is not necessarily and in every sense borne out by the results. The rationalist attitude may go to work with information and technique so inadequate that actions—and especially a general surgical propensity— induced by it may, to an observer of a later period, appear to be, even from a purely intellectual standpoint, inferior to the actions and anti-surgical propensities associated with attitudes that at the time most people felt inclined to attribute to a low I.Q. A large part of the political thought of the seventeenth and eighteenth centuries illustrates this ever-forgotten truth. Not only in depth of social vision but also in logical analysis later "conservative" countercriticism was clearly superior although it would have been a mere matter of laughter for the writers of the enlightenment.

Now the rational attitude presumably forced itself on the human mind primarily from economic necessity; it is the everyday economic task to which we as a race owe our elementary training in rational thought and behavior—I have no hesitation in saying that all logic is

[3] This Kantian phrase has been chosen in order to guard against an obvious objection.

derived from the pattern of the economic decision or, to use a pet phrase of mine, that the economic pattern is the matrix of logic. This seems plausible for the following reason. Suppose that some "primitive" man uses that most elementary of all machines, already appreciated by our gorilla cousins, a stick, and that this stick breaks in his hand. If he tries to remedy the damage by reciting a magic formula—he might for instance murmur Supply and Demand or Planning and Control in the expectation that if he repeats this exactly nine times the two fragments will unite again—then he is within the precincts of pre-rational thought. If he gropes for the best way to join the fragments or to procure another stick, he is being rational in our sense. Both attitudes are possible of course. But it stands to reason that in this and most other economic actions the failure of a magic formula to work will be much more obvious than could be any failure of a formula that was to make our man victorious in combat or lucky in love or to lift a load of guilt from his conscience. This is due to the inexorable definiteness and, in most cases, the quantitative character that distinguish the economic from other spheres of human action, perhaps also to the unemotional drabness of the unending rhythm of economic wants and satisfactions. Once hammered in, the rational habit spreads under the pedagogic influence of favorable experiences to the other spheres and there also opens eyes for that amazing thing, the Fact.

This process is independent of any particular garb, hence also of the capitalistic garb, of economic activity. So is the profit motive and self-interest. Pre-capitalist man is in fact no less "grabbing" than capitalist man. Peasant serfs for instance or warrior lords assert their self-interest with a brutal energy all their own. But capitalism develops rationality and adds a new edge to it in two interconnected ways.

First it exalts the monetary unit—not itself a creation of capitalism—into a unit of account. That is to say, capitalist practice turns the unit of money into a tool of rational cost-profit calculations, of which the towering monument is double-entry bookkeeping.[4] Without going into this, we will notice that, primarily a product of the evolution of economic rationality, the cost-profit calculus in turn reacts upon that rationality; by crystallizing and defining numerically, it powerfully propels the logic of enterprise. And thus defined and quantified

---

[4] This element has been stressed, and *more suo* overstressed, by Sombart. Double-entry bookkeeping is the last step on a long and tortuous road. Its immediate predecessor was the practice of making up from time to time an inventory and figuring out profit or loss; see A. Sapori in *Biblioteca Storica Toscana*, VII, 1932. Luca Pacioli's treatise on bookkeeping, 1494, supplies by its date an important milestone. For the history and sociology of the state it is a vital fact to notice that rational bookkeeping did not intrude into the management of public funds until the eighteenth century and that even then it did so imperfectly and in the primitive form of "cameralist" bookkeeping.

for the economic sector, this type of logic or attitude or method then starts upon its conqueror's career subjugating—rationalizing—man's tools and philosophies, his medical practice, his picture of the cosmos, his outlook on life, everything in fact including his concepts of beauty and justice and his spiritual ambitions.

In this respect it is highly significant that modern mathematico-experimental science developed, in the fifteenth, sixteenth and seventeenth centuries, not only along with the social process usually referred to as the Rise of Capitalism, but also outside of the fortress of scholastic thought and in the face of its contemptuous hostility. In the fifteenth century mathematics was mainly concerned with questions of commercial arithmetic and the problems of the architect. The utilitarian mechanical device, invented by men of the craftsman type, stood at the source of modern physics. The rugged individualism of Galileo was the individualism of the rising capitalist class. The surgeon began to rise above the midwife and the barber. The artist who at the same time was an engineer and an entrepreneur—the type immortalized by such men as Vinci, Alberti, Cellini; even Dürer busied himself with plans for fortifications—illustrates best of all what I mean. By cursing it all, scholastic professors in the Italian universities showed more sense than we give them credit for. The trouble was not with individual unorthodox propositions. Any decent schoolman could be trusted to twist his texts so as to fit the Copernican system. But those professors quite rightly sensed the spirit behind such exploits—the spirit of rationalist individualism, the spirit generated by rising capitalism.

Second, rising capitalism produced not only the mental attitude of modern science, the attitude that consists in asking certain questions and in going about answering them in a certain way, but also the men and the means. By breaking up the feudal environment and disturbing the intellectual peace of manor and village (though there always was, of course, plenty to discuss and to fall out about in a convent), but especially by creating the social space for a new class that stood upon individual achievement in the economic field, it in turn attracted to that field the strong wills and the strong intellects. Precapitalist economic life left no scope for achievement that would carry over class boundaries or, to put it differently, be adequate to create social positions comparable to those of the members of the then ruling classes. Not that it precluded ascent in general.[5] But business activity was, broadly speaking, essentially subordinate, even at the peak of success within the craft guild, and it hardly ever led out of it. The

[5] We are too prone to look upon the medieval social structure as static or rigid. As a matter of fact, there was an incessant—to use Pareto's term—*circulation des aristocracies*. The elements that composed the uppermost stratum around 900 had practically disappeared by 1500.

main avenues to advancement and large gain were the church—nearly as accessible throughout the Middle Ages as it is now—to which we may add the chanceries of the great territorial magnates, and the hierarchy of warrior lords—quite accessible to every man who was physically and psychically fit until about the middle of the twelfth century, and not quite inaccessible thereafter. It was only when capitalist enterprise—first commercial and financial, then mining, finally industrial—unfolded its possibilities that supernormal ability and ambition began to turn to business as a third avenue. Success was quick and conspicuous, but it has been much exaggerated as regards the social weight it carried at first. If we look closely at the career of Jacob Fugger, for instance, or of Agostino Chigi, we easily satisfy ourselves that they had very little to do with steering the policies of Charles V or of Pope Leo X and that they paid heavily for such privileges as they enjoyed.[6] Yet entrepreneurial success was fascinating enough for everyone excepting the highest strata of feudal society to draw most of the best brains and thus to generate further success—to generate additional steam for the rationalist engine. So, in this sense, capitalism—and not merely economic activity in general—has after all been the propelling force of the rationalization of human behavior.

And now we are at long last face to face with the immediate goal[7] to which that complex yet inadequate argument was to lead. Not only the modern mechanized plant and the volume of the output that pours forth from it, not only modern technology and economic organization, but all the features and achievements of modern civilization are, directly or indirectly, the products of the capitalist process. They must be included in any balance sheet of it and in any verdict about its deeds or misdeeds.

There is the growth of rational science and the long list of its applications. Airplanes, refrigerators, television and that sort of thing are immediately recognizable as results of the profit economy. But although the modern hospital is not as a rule operated for profit, it is nonetheless the product of capitalism not only, to repeat, because the capitalist process supplies the means and the will, but much more fundamentally because capitalist rationality supplied the habits of

---

[6] The Medici are not really an exception. For though their wealth helped them to acquire control of the Florentine commonwealth, it was this control and not the wealth *per se* which accounts for the role played by the family. In any case they are the only merchants that ever rose to a footing of equality with the uppermost stratum of the feudal world. Real exceptions we find only where capitalist evolution *created* an environment or completely broke up the feudal stratum—in Venice and in the Netherlands for instance.

[7] The *immediate* goal, because the analysis contained in the last pages will stand us in good stead also for other purposes. It is in fact fundamental for any serious discussion of the great theme of Capitalism and Socialism.

mind that evolved the methods used in these hospitals. And the victories, not yet completely won but in the offing, over cancer, syphilis and tuberculosis will be as much capitalist achievements as motorcars or pipe lines or Bessemer steel have been. In the case of medicine, there is a capitalist profession behind the methods, capitalist both because to a large extent it works in a business spirit and because it is an emulsion of the industrial and commercial bourgeoisie. But even if that were not so, modern medicine and hygiene would still be by-products of the capitalist process just as is modern education.

There is the capitalist art and the capitalist style of life. If we limit ourselves to painting as an example, both for brevity's sake and because in that field my ignorance is slightly less complete than it is in others, and if (wrongly, as I think) we agree to start an epoch with Giotto's Arena frescoes and then follow the line (nothing short of damnable though such "linear" arguments are) Giotto—Masaccio—Vinci—Michelangelo—Greco, no amount of emphasis on mystical ardors in the case of Greco can obliterate my point for anyone who has eyes that see. And Vinci's experiments are offered to doubters who wish, as it were, to touch the capitalist rationality with their fingertips. This line if projected (yes, I know) could be made to land us (though perhaps gasping) in the contrast between Delacroix and Ingres. Well, and there we are; Cézanne, Van Gogh, Picasso or Matisse will do the rest. Expressionist liquidation of the object forms an admirably logical conclusion. The story of the capitalist novel (culminating in the Goncourt novel: "documents written up") would illustrate still better. But that is obvious. The evolution of the capitalist style of life could be easily—and perhaps most tellingly—described in terms of the genesis of the modern lounge suit.

There is finally all that may be grouped around the symbolic centerpiece of Gladstonian liberalism. The term Individualist Democracy would do just as well—better in fact because we want to cover some things that Gladstone would not have approved and a moral and spiritual attitude which, dwelling in the citadel of faith, he actually hated. At that I could leave this point if radical liturgy did not consist largely in picturesque denials of what I mean to convey. Radicals may insist that the masses are crying for salvation from intolerable sufferings and rattling their chains in darkness and despair, but of course there never was so much personal freedom of mind and body for all, never so much readiness to bear with and even to finance the mortal enemies of the leading class, never so much active sympathy with real and faked sufferings, never so much readiness to accept burdens, as there is in modern capitalist society; and whatever democracy there was, outside of peasant communities, developed historically in the wake of both modern and ancient capitalism. Again plenty of facts can be adduced from the past to make up a counterargument

that will be effective but is irrelevant in a discussion of present conditions and future alternatives.[8] If we do decide to embark upon historical disquisition at all, then even many of those facts which to
radical critics may seem to be the most eligible ones for their purpose
will often look differently if viewed in the light of a comparison with
the corresponding facts of pre-capitalist experience. And it cannot be
replied that "those were different times." For it is precisely the capitalist process that made the difference.

Two points in particular must be mentioned. I have pointed out
before that social legislation or, more generally, institutional change
for the benefit of the masses is not simply something which has been
forced upon capitalist society by an ineluctable necessity to alleviate
the ever-deepening misery of the poor but that, besides raising the
standard of living of the masses by virtue of its automatic effects, the
capitalist process also provided for that legislation the means "and
the will." The words in quotes require further explanation that is to
be found in the principle of spreading rationality. The capitalist
process rationalizes behavior and ideas and by so doing chases from
our minds, along with metaphysical belief, mystic and romantic ideas
of all sorts. Thus it reshapes not only our methods of attaining our
ends but also these ultimate ends themselves. "Free thinking" in the
sense of materialistic monism, laicism and pragmatic acceptance of
the world this side of the grave follow from this not indeed by logical
necessity but nevertheless very naturally. On the one hand, our inherited sense of duty, deprived of its traditional basis, becomes focused
in utilitarian ideas about the betterment of mankind which, quite
illogically to be sure, seem to withstand rationalist criticism better
than, say, the fear of God does. On the other hand, the same rationalization of the soul rubs off all the glamour of super-empirical sanction
from every species of classwise rights. This then, together with the
typically capitalist enthusiasm for Efficiency and Service—so completely different from the body of ideas which would have been associated with those terms by the typical knight of old—breeds that
"will" within the bourgeoisie itself. Feminism, an essentially capitalist
phenomenon, illustrates the point still more clearly. The reader will
realize that these tendencies must be understood "objectively" and
that therefore no amount of anti-feminist or anti-reformist *talk* or
even of temporary opposition to any particular measure proves anything against this analysis. These things are the very symptoms of the
tendencies they pretend to fight. Of this, more in the subsequent
chapters.

Also, capitalist civilization is rationalistic "and anti-heroic." The

[8] Even Marx, in whose time indictments of this kind were not anything like as
absurd as they are today, evidently thought it desirable to strengthen his case by
dwelling on conditions that even then were either past or visibly passing.

two go together of course. Success in industry and commerce requires a lot of stamina, yet industrial and commercial activity is essentially unheroic in the knight's sense—no flourishing of swords about it, not much physical prowess, no chance to gallop the armored horse into the enemy, preferably a heretic or heathen—and the ideology that glorifies the idea of fighting for fighting's sake and of victory for victory's sake understandably withers in the office among all the columns of figures. Therefore, owning assets that are apt to attract the robber or the tax gatherer and not sharing or even disliking warrior ideology that conflicts with its "rational" utilitarianism, the industrial and commercial bourgeoisie is fundamentally pacifist and inclined to insist on the application of the moral precepts of private life to international relations. It is true that, unlike most but like some other features of capitalist civilization, pacifism and international morality have also been espoused in non-capitalist environments and by precapitalist agencies, in the Middle Ages by the Roman Church for instance. Modern pacifism and modern international morality are nonetheless products of capitalism.

In view of the fact that Marxian doctrine—especially Neo-Marxian doctrine and even a considerable body of non-socialist opinion—is, as we have seen in the first part of this book, strongly opposed to this proposition it is necessary to point out that the latter is not meant to deny that many a bourgeoisie has put up a splendid fight for hearth and home, or that almost purely bourgeois commonwealths were often aggressive when it seemed to pay—like the Athenian or the Venetian commonwealths—or that no bourgeoisie ever disliked war profits and advantages to trade accruing from conquest or refused to be trained in warlike nationalism by its feudal masters or leaders or by the propaganda of some specially interested group. All I hold is, first, that such instances of capitalist combativeness are not, as Marxism has it, to be explained—exclusively or primarily—in terms of class interests or class situations that systematically engender capitalist wars of conquest; second, that there is a difference between doing that which you consider your normal business in life, for which you prepare yourself in season and out of season and in terms of which you define your success or failure, and doing what is not in your line, for which your normal work and your mentality do not fit you and success in which will increase the prestige of the most unbourgeois of professions; and third, that this difference steadily tells—in international as well as in domestic affairs—against the use of military force and for peaceful arrangements, even where the balance of pecuniary advantage is clearly on the side of war which, under modern circumstances, is not in general very likely. As a matter of fact, the more completely capitalist the structure and attitude of a nation, the more pacifist—and the more prone to count the costs of war—we observe it to be. Owing to the complex nature of every individual pattern, this could be fully brought out only by detailed historical analysis. But the bourgeois attitude to the military (standing armies), the spirit in which and the methods by which bourgeois societies wage war, and the readiness with which, in any serious case of prolonged warfare, they submit to non-bourgeois rule are conclusive in themselves. The Marxist theory that imperialism is the last stage of capitalist evolution therefore fails quite irrespective of purely economic objections.

But I am not going to sum up as the reader presumably expects me to. That is to say, I am not going to invite him, before he decides to put his trust in an untried alternative advocated by untried men, to look once more at the impressive economic and the still more impressive cultural achievement of the capitalist order and at the immense promise held out by both. I am not going to argue that that achievement and that promise are in themselves sufficient to support an argument for allowing the capitalist process to work on and, as it might easily be put, to lift poverty from the shoulders of mankind.

There would be no sense in this. Even if mankind were as free to choose as a businessman is free to choose between two competing pieces of machinery, no determined value judgment necessarily follows from the facts and relations between facts that I have tried to convey. As regards the economic performance, it does not follow that men are "happier" or even "better off" in the industrial society of today than they were in a medieval manor or village. As regards the cultural performance, one may accept every word I have written and yet hate it— its utilitarianism and the wholesale destruction of Meanings incident to it—from the bottom of one's heart. Moreover, as I shall have to emphasize again in our discussion of the socialist alternative, one may care less for the efficiency of the capitalist process in producing economic and cultural values than for the kind of human beings that it turns out and then leaves to their own devices, free to make a mess of their lives. There is a type of radical whose adverse verdict about capitalist civilization rests on nothing except stupidity, ignorance or irresponsibility, who is unable or unwilling to grasp the most obvious facts, let alone their wider implications. But a completely adverse verdict may also be arrived at on a higher plane.

However, whether favorable or unfavorable, value judgments about capitalist performance are of little interest. For mankind is not free to choose. This is not only because the mass of people are not in a position to compare alternatives rationally and always accept what they are being told. There is a much deeper reason for it. Things economic and social move by their own momentum and the ensuing situations compel individuals and groups to behave in certain ways whatever they may wish to do—not indeed by destroying their free-

dom of choice but by shaping the choosing mentalities and by nar-
rowing the list of possibilities from which to choose. If this is the
quintessence of Marxism then we all of us have got to be Marxists. In
consequence, capitalist performance is not even relevant for prognosis.
Most civilizations have disappeared before they had time to fill to
the full the measure of their promise. Hence I am not going to argue,
on the strength of that performance, that the capitalist intermezzo is
likely to be prolonged. In fact, I am now going to draw the exactly
opposite inference.

VIII

CRUMBLING WALLS

I. The Obsolescence of the Entrepreneurial Function

In our discussion of the theory of vanishing investment opportunity, a reservation was made in favor of the possibility that the economic wants of humanity might some day be so completely satisfied that little motive would be left to push productive effort still further ahead. Such a state of satiety is no doubt very far off even if we keep within the present scheme of wants; and if we take account of the fact that, as higher standards of life are attained, these wants automatically expand and new wants emerge or are created,[1] satiety becomes a flying goal, particularly if we include leisure among consumers' goods. However, let us glance at that possibility, assuming, still more unrealistically, that methods of production have reached a state of perfection which does not admit of further improvement.

A more or less stationary state would ensue. Capitalism, being essentially an evolutionary process, would become atrophic. There would be nothing left for entrepreneurs to do. They would find themselves in much the same situation as generals would in a society perfectly sure of permanent peace. Profits and along with profits the rate of interest would converge toward zero. The bourgeois strata that live on profits and interest would tend to disappear. The management of industry and trade would become a matter of current administration, and the personnel would unavoidably acquire the characteristics of a bureaucracy. Socialism of a very sober type would almost automatically come into being. Human energy would turn away from business. Other than economic pursuits would attract the brains and provide the adventure.

For the calculable future this vision is of no importance. But all the greater importance attaches to the fact that many of the effects on the structure of society and on the organization of the productive process that we might expect from an approximately complete satisfaction of wants or from absolute technological perfection can also be expected from a development that is clearly observable already. Progress itself may be mechanized as well as the management of a stationary economy, and this mechanization of progress may affect entrepreneurship and capitalist society nearly as much as the cessation of economic progress would. In order to see this it is only necessary to restate,

[1] Wilhelm Wundt called this the Heterogony of Aims (*Heterogonie der Zwecke*).

first, what the entrepreneurial function consists in and, secondly, what it means for bourgeois society and the survival of the capitalist order.

We have seen that the function of entrepreneurs is to reform or revolutionize the pattern of production by exploiting an invention or, more generally, an untried technological possibility for producing a new commodity or producing an old one in a new way, by opening up a new source of supply of materials or a new outlet for products, by reorganizing an industry and so on. Railroad construction in its earlier stages, electrical power production before the First World War, steam and steel, the motorcar, colonial ventures afford spectacular instances of a large genus which comprises innumerable humbler ones —down to such things as making a success of a particular kind of sausage or toothbrush. This kind of activity is primarily responsible for the recurrent "prosperities" that revolutionize the economic organism and the recurrent "recessions" that are due to the disequilibrating impact of the new products or methods. To undertake such new things is difficult and constitutes a distinct economic function, first, because they lie outside of the routine tasks which everybody understands and, secondly, because the environment resists in many ways that vary, according to social conditions, from simple refusal either to finance or to buy a new thing, to physical attack on the man who tries to produce it. To act with confidence beyond the range of familiar beacons and to overcome that resistance requires aptitudes that are present in only a small fraction of the population and that define the entrepreneurial type as well as the entrepreneurial function. This function does not essentially consist in either inventing anything or otherwise creating the conditions which the enterprise exploits. It consists in getting things done.

This social function is already losing importance and is bound to lose it at an accelerating rate in the future even if the economic process itself of which entrepreneurship was the prime mover went on unabated. For, on the one hand, it is much easier now than it has been in the past to do things that lie outside familiar routine—innovation itself is being reduced to routine. Technological progress is increasingly becoming the business of teams of trained specialists who turn out what is required and make it work in predictable ways. The romance of earlier commercial adventure is rapidly wearing away, because so many more things can be strictly calculated that had of old to be visualized in a flash of genius.

On the other hand, personality and will power must count for less in environments which have become accustomed to economic change— best instanced by an incessant stream of new consumers' and producers' goods—and which, instead of resisting, accept it as a matter of course. The resistance which comes from interests threatened by an innovation in the productive process is not likely to die out as long as the capitalist order persists. It is, for instance, the great obstacle on the road toward mass production of cheap housing which presupposes radical mechanization and wholesale elimination of inefficient methods of work on the plot. But every other kind of resistance—the resistance, in particular, of consumers and producers to a new kind of thing because it is new—has well-nigh vanished already.

Thus, economic progress tends to become depersonalized and automatized. Bureau and committee work tends to replace individual action. Once more, reference to the military analogy will help to bring out the essential point.

Of old, roughly up to and including the Napoleonic Wars, generalship meant leadership and success meant the personal success of the man in command who earned corresponding "profits" in terms of social prestige. The technique of warfare and the structure of armies being what they were, the individual decision and driving power of the leading man—even his actual presence on a showy horse—were essential elements in the strategical and tactical situations. Napoleon's presence was, and had to be, actually felt on his battlefields. This is no longer so. Rationalized and specialized office work will eventually blot out personality, the calculable result, the "vision." The leading man no longer has the opportunity to fling himself into the fray. He is becoming just another office worker—and one who is not always difficult to replace.

Or take another military analogy. Warfare in the Middle Ages was a very personal affair. The armored knights practiced an art that required lifelong training and every one of them counted individually by virtue of personal skill and prowess. It is easy to understand why this craft should have become the basis of a social class in the fullest and richest sense of that term. But social and technological change undermined and eventually destroyed both the function and the position of that class. Warfare itself did not cease on that account. It simply became more and more mechanized—eventually so much so that success in what now is a mere profession no longer carries that connotation of individual achievement which would raise not only the man but also his group into a durable position of social leadership.

Now a similar social process—in the last analysis the same social process—undermines the role and, along with the role, the social position of the capitalist entrepreneur. His role, though less glamorous than that of medieval warlords, great or small, also is or was just another form of individual leadership acting by virtue of personal force and personal responsibility for success. His position, like that of warrior classes, is threatened as soon as this function in the social process loses its importance, and no less if this is due to the cessation of the social needs it served than if those needs are being served by other, more impersonal, methods.

But this affects the position of the entire bourgeois stratum. Although entrepreneurs are not necessarily or even typically elements of that stratum from the outset, they nevertheless enter it in case of success. Thus, though entrepreneurs do not *per se* form a social class, the bourgeois class absorbs them and their families and connections, thereby recruiting and revitalizing itself currently while at the same time the families that sever their active relation to "business" drop out of it after a generation or two. Between, there is the bulk of what we refer to as industrialists, merchants, financiers and bankers; they are in the intermediate stage between entrepreneurial venture and mere current administration of an inherited domain. The returns on which the class lives are produced by, and the social position of the class rests on, the success of this more or less active sector—which of course may, as it does in this country, form over 90 per cent of the bourgeois stratum—and of the individuals who are in the act of rising into that class. Economically and sociologically, directly and indirectly, the bourgeoisie therefore depends on the entrepreneur and, as a class, lives and will die with him, though a more or less prolonged transitional stage—eventually a stage in which it may feel equally unable to die and to live—is quite likely to occur, as in fact it did occur in the case of the feudal civilization.

To sum up this part of our argument: if capitalist evolution—"progress"—either ceases or becomes completely automatic, the economic basis of the industrial bourgeoisie will be reduced eventually to wages such as are paid for current administrative work excepting remnants of quasi-rents and monopoloid gains that may be expected to linger on for some time. Since capitalist enterprise, by its very achievements, tends to automatize progress, we conclude that it tends to make itself superfluous—to break to pieces under the pressure of its own success. The perfectly bureaucratized giant industrial unit not only ousts the small or medium-sized firm and "expropriates" its owners, but in the end it also ousts the entrepreneur and expropriates the bourgeoisie as a class which in the process stands to lose not only its income but also what is infinitely more important, its function. The true pacemakers of socialism were not the intellectuals or agitators who preached it but the Vanderbilts, Carnegies and Rockefellers. This result may not in every respect be to the taste of Marxian socialists, still less to the taste of socialists of a more popular (Marx would have said, vulgar) description. But so far as prognosis goes, it does not differ from theirs.

II. The Destruction of the Protecting Strata

So far we have been considering the effects of the capitalist process upon the economic bases of the upper strata of capitalist society and upon their social position and prestige. But effects further extend to the institutional framework that protected them. In showing this we shall take the term in its widest acceptance so as to include not only legal institutions but also attitudes of the public mind and policies.

1. Capitalist evolution first of all destroyed, or went far toward destroying, the institutional arrangements of the feudal world—the manor, the village, the craft guild. The facts and mechanisms of this process are too familiar to detain us. Destruction was wrought in three ways. The world of the artisan was destroyed primarily by the automatic effects of the competition that came from the capitalist entrepreneur; political action in removing atrophic organizations and regulations only registered results. The world of the lord and the peasant was destroyed primarily by political—in some cases revolutionary—action and capitalism merely presided over adaptive transformations say, of the German manorial organizations into large-scale agricultural units of production. But along with these industrial and agrarian revolutions went a no less revolutionary change in the general attitude of legislative authority and public opinion. Together with the old economic organization vanished the economic and political privileges of the classes or groups that used to play the leading role in it, particularly the tax exemptions and the political prerogatives of the landed nobility and gentry and of the clergy.

Economically all this meant for the bourgeoisie the breaking of so many fetters and the removal of so many barriers. Politically it meant the replacement of an order in which the bourgeois was a humble subject by another that was more congenial to his rationalist mind and to his immediate interests. But, surveying that process from the standpoint of today, the observer might well wonder whether in the end such complete emancipation was good for the bourgeois and his world. For those fetters not only hampered, they also sheltered. Before proceeding further we must carefully clarify and appraise this point.

2. The related processes of the rise of the capitalist bourgeoisie and of the rise of national states produced, in the sixteenth, seventeenth and eighteenth centuries, a social structure that may seem to us amphibial though it was no more amphibial or transitional than any other. Consider the outstanding instance that is afforded by the monarchy of Louis XIV. The royal power had subjugated the landed aristocracy and at the same time conciliated it by proffering employment and pensions and by conditionally accepting its claim to a ruling or leading class position. The same royal power had subjugated and allied itself with the clergy.[2] It had finally strengthened its sway over the bourgeoisie, its old ally in the struggle with the territorial magnates, protecting and propelling its enterprise in order to exploit it the more effectively in turn. Peasants and the (small) industrial proletariat were

[2] Gallicanism was nothing else but the ideological reflex of this.

likewise managed, exploited and protected by public authority—though the protection was in the case of the French *ancien régime* very much less in evidence than for instance in the Austria of Maria. Theresa or of Joseph II—and, vicariously, by landlords or industrialists. This was not simply a government in the sense of nineteenth-century liberalism, i.e., a social agency existing for the performance of a few limited functions to be financed by a minimum of revenue. On principle, the monarchy managed everything, from consciences to the patterns of the silk fabrics of Lyons, and financially it aimed at a maximum of revenue. Though the king was never really absolute, public authority was all-comprehensive.

Correct diagnosis of this pattern is of the utmost importance for our subject. The king, the court, the army, the church and the bureaucracy lived to an increasing extent on revenue created by the capitalist process, even purely feudal sources of income being swelled in consequence of contemporaneous capitalist developments. To an increasing extent also, domestic and foreign policies and institutional changes were shaped to suit and propel that development. *As far as that goes,* the feudal elements in the structure of the so-called absolute monarchy come in only under the heading of atavisms which in fact is the diagnosis one would naturally adopt at first sight.

Looking more closely, however, we realize that those elements meant more than that. The steel frame of that structure still consisted of the human material of feudal society and this material still behaved according to precapitalist patterns. It filled the offices of state, officered the army, devised policies—it functioned as a *classe dirigente* and, though taking account of bourgeois interests, it took care to distance itself from the bourgeoisie. The centerpiece, the king, was king by the grace of God, and the root of his position was feudal, not only in the historical but also in the sociological sense, however much he availed himself of the economic possibilities offered by capitalism. All this was more than atavism. It was an active symbiosis of two social strata, one of which no doubt supported the other economically but was in turn supported by the other politically. Whatever we may think of the achievements or shortcomings of this arrangement, whatever the bourgeois himself may have thought of it at the time or later—and of the aristocratic scapegrace or idler—it was of the essence of that society.

3. Of *that* society only? The subsequent course of things, best exemplified by the English case, suggests the answer. The aristocratic element continued to rule the roost *right to the end of the period of intact and vital capitalism.* No doubt that element—though nowhere so effectively as in England—currently absorbed the brains from other strata that drifted into politics; it made itself the representative of bourgeois interests and fought the battles of the bourgeoisie; it

had to surrender its last legal privileges; but with these qualifications, and for ends no longer its own, it continued to man the political engine, to manage the state, to govern.

The economically operative part of the bourgeois strata did not offer much opposition to this. On the whole, that kind of division of labor suited them and they liked it. Where they did revolt against it or where they got into the political saddle without having to revolt, they did not make a conspicuous success of ruling and did not prove able to hold their own. The question arises whether it is really safe to assume that these failures were merely due to lack of opportunity to acquire experience and, with experience, the attitudes of a politically ruling class.

It is not. There is a more fundamental reason for those failures such as are instanced by the French or German experiences with bourgeois attempts at ruling—a reason which again will best be visualized by contrasting the figure of the industrialist or merchant with that of the medieval lord. The latter's "profession" not only qualified him admirably for the defense of his own class interest— he was not only able to fight for it physically—but it also cast a halo around him and made of him a ruler of men. The first was important, but more so were the mystic glamour and the lordly attitude— that ability and habit to command and to be obeyed that carried prestige with all classes of society and in every walk of life. That prestige was so great and that attitude so useful that the class position outlived the social and technological conditions which had given rise to it and proved adaptable, by means of a transformation of the class function, to quite different social and economic conditions. With the utmost ease and grace the lords and knights metamorphosed themselves into courtiers, administrators, diplomats, politicians and into military officers of a type that had nothing whatever to do with that of the medieval knight. And—most astonishing phenomenon when we come to think of it—a remnant of that old prestige survives even to this day, and not only with our ladies.

Of the industrialist and merchant the opposite is true. There is surely no trace of any mystic glamour about him which is what counts in the ruling of men. The stock exchange is a poor substitute for the Holy Grail. We have seen that the industrialist and merchant, as far as they are entrepreneurs, also fill a function of leadership. But economic leadership of this type does not readily expand, like the medieval lord's military leadership, into the leadership of nations. On the contrary, the ledger and the cost calculation absorb and confine.

I have called the bourgeois rationalist and unheroic. He can only use rationalist and unheroic means to defend his position or to bend a nation to his will. He can impress by what people may expect from his economic performance, he can argue his case, he can promise to pay out money or threaten to withhold it, he can hire the treacherous services of a *condottiere* or politician or journalist. But that is all and all of it is greatly overrated as to its political value. Nor are his experiences and habits of life of the kind that develop personal fascination. A genius in the business office may be, and often is, utterly unable outside of it to say boo to a goose—both in the drawing room and on the platform. Knowing this he wants to be left alone and to leave politics alone.

Again exceptions will occur to the reader. But again they do not amount to much. Aptitude for, and interest and success in, city management is the only important exception in Europe, and this will be found to strengthen our case instead of weakening it. Before the advent of the modern metropolis, which is no longer a bourgeois affair, city management was akin to business management. Grasp of its problems and authority within its precincts came naturally to the manufacturer and trader, and the local interests of manufacturing and trading supplied most of the subject matter of its politics which therefore lent itself to treatment by the methods and in the spirit of the business office. Under exceptionally favorable conditions, exceptional developments sprouted from those roots, such as the developments of the Venetian or Genoese republics. The case of the Low Countries enters into the same pattern, but it is particularly instructive by virtue of the fact that the merchants' republic invariably failed in the great game of international politics and that in practically every emergency it had to hand over the reins to a warlord of feudal complexion. As regards the United States, it would be easy to list the uniquely favorable circumstances—rapidly waning —that explain its case.

4. The inference is obvious: barring such exceptional conditions, the bourgeois class is ill equipped to face the problems, both domestic and international, that have normally to be faced by a country of any importance. The bourgeois themselves feel this in spite of all the phraseology that seems to deny it, and so do the masses. Within a protecting framework not made of bourgeois material, the bourgeoisie may be successful, not only in the political defensive but also in the offensive, especially as an opposition. For a time it felt so safe as to be able to afford the luxury of attacking the protective frame itself; such bourgeois opposition as there was in imperial Germany illustrates this to perfection. But without protection by some non-bourgeois group, the bourgeoisie is politically helpless and unable not only to lead its nation but even to take care of its particular class interest. Which amounts to saying that it needs a master.

But the capitalist process, both by its economic mechanics and by its psycho-sociological effects, did away with this protecting master or, as in this country, never gave him, or a substitute for him, a chance to develop. The implications of this are strengthened by another consequence of the same process. Capitalist evolution eliminates not only the king *Dei Gratia* but also the political entrenchments that, had they proved tenable, would have been formed by the village and the craft guild. Of course, neither organization was tenable in the precise shape in which capitalism found it. But capitalist policies wrought destruction much beyond what was unavoidable. They attacked the artisan in reservations in which he could have survived for an indefinite time. They forced upon the peasant all the blessings of early liberalism—the free and unsheltered holding and all the individualist rope he needed in order to hang himself.

In breaking down the pre-capitalist framework of society, capitalism thus broke not only barriers that impeded its progress but also flying buttresses that prevented its collapse. That process, impressive in its relentless necessity, was not merely a matter of removing institutional deadwood, but of removing partners of the capitalist stratum, symbiosis with whom was an essential element of the capitalist schema. Having discovered this fact which so many slogans obscure, we might well wonder whether it is quite correct to look upon capitalism as a social form *sui generis* or, in fact, as anything else but the last stage of the decomposition of what we have called feudalism. On the whole, I am inclined to believe that its peculiarities suffice to make a type and to accept that symbiosis of classes which owe their existence to different epochs and processes as the rule rather than as an exception —at least it has been the rule these 6000 years, i.e., ever since primitive tillers of the soil became the subjects of mounted nomads. But there is no great objection that I can see against the opposite view alluded to.

III. The Destruction of the Institutional Framework of Capitalist Society

We return from our digression with a load of ominous facts. They are almost, though not quite, sufficient to establish our next point, viz., that the capitalist process in much the same way in which it destroyed the institutional framework of feudal society also undermines its own.

It has been pointed out above that the very success of capitalist enterprise paradoxically tends to impair the prestige or social weight of the class primarily associated with it and that the giant unit of control tends to oust the bourgeoisie from the function to which it owed that social weight. The corresponding change in the meaning, and the incidental loss in vitality, of the institutions of the bourgeois world and of its typical attitudes are easy to trace.

On the one hand, the capitalist process unavoidably attacks the economic standing ground of the small producer and trader. What it did to the pre-capitalist strata it also does—and by the same competitive mechanism—to the lower strata of capitalist industry. Here of course Marx scores. It is true that the facts of industrial concentration do not quite live up to the ideas the public is being taught to entertain about it. The process has gone less far and is less free from setbacks and compensatory tendencies than one would gather from many a popular exposition. In particular, large-scale enterprise not only annihilates but also, to some extent, creates space for the small producing, and especially trading, firm. Also, in the case of the peasants and farmers, the capitalist world has at last proved both willing and able to pursue an expensive but on the whole effective policy of conservation. In the long run, however, there can be little doubt about the fact we are envisaging, or about its consequences. Outside of the agrarian field, moreover, the bourgeoisie has shown but little awareness of the problem[3] or its importance for the survival of the capitalist order. The profits to be made by rationalizing the organization of production and especially by cheapening the tortuous way of commodities from the factory to the ultimate consumer are more than the mind of the typical businessman can resist.

Now it is important to realize precisely what these consequences consist in. A very common type of social criticism which we have already met laments the "decline of competition" and equates it to the decline of capitalism because of the virtues it attributes to competition and the vices it attributes to modern industrial "monopolies." In this schema of interpretation, monopolization plays the role of arteriosclerosis and reacts upon the fortunes of the capitalist order through increasingly unsatisfactory economic performance. We have seen the reasons for rejecting this view. Economically neither the case for competition nor the case against concentration of economic control is anything like as strong as this argument implies. And, whether weak or strong, it misses the salient point. Even if the giant concerns were all managed so perfectly as to call forth applause from the angels in heaven, the political consequences of concentration would still be what they are. The political structure of a nation is profoundly affected by the elimination of a host of small and medium-sized firms the owner-managers of which, together with their dependents, henchmen and connections, count quantitatively at the polls and have a hold on what we may term the foreman class that no management of a large unit can ever have; the very foundation of private property and free contracting wears away in a nation in

---

[3] Although some governments did; the government of imperial Germany did much to fight this particular kind of rationalization, and there is now a strong tendency to do the same in this country.

which its most vital, most concrete, most meaningful types disappear from the moral horizon of the people.

On the other hand, the capitalist process also attacks its own institutional framework—let us continue to visualize "property" and "free contracting" as *partes pro toto*—within the precincts of the big units. Excepting the cases that are still of considerable importance in which a corporation is practically owned by a single individual or family, the figure of the proprietor and with it the specifically proprietary interest have vanished from the picture. There are the salaried executives and all the salaried managers and submanagers. There are the big stockholders. And then there are the small stockholders. The first group tends to acquire the employee attitude and rarely if ever identifies itself with the stockholding interest even in the most favorable cases, i.e., in the cases in which it identifies itself with the interest of the concern as such. The second group, even if it considers its connection with the concern as permanent and even if it actually behaves as financial theory would have stockholders behave, is at one remove from both the functions and the attitudes of an owner. As to the third group, small stockholders often do not care much about what for most of them is but a minor source of income and, whether they care or not, they hardly ever bother, unless they or some representatives of theirs are out to exploit their nuisance value; being often very ill used and still more often thinking themselves ill used, they almost regularly drift into an attitude hostile to "their" corporations, to big business in general and, particularly when things look bad, to the capitalist order as such. No element of any of those three groups into which I schematized the typical situation unconditionally takes the attitude characteristic of that curious phenomenon, so full of meaning and so rapidly passing, that is covered by the term Property.

Freedom of contracting is in the same boat. In its full vitality it meant individual contracting regulated by individual choice between an indefinite number of possibilities. The stereotyped, unindividual, impersonal and bureaucratized contract of today—this applies much more generally, but *a potiori* we may fasten upon the labor contract —which presents but restricted freedom of choice and mostly turns on a *c'est à prendre ou à laisser*, has none of the old features the most important of which become impossible with giant concerns dealing with other giant concerns or impersonal masses of workmen or consumers. The void is being filled by a tropical growth of new legal structures—and a little reflection shows that this could hardly be otherwise.

Thus the capitalist process pushes into the background all those institutions, the institutions of property and free contracting in particular, that expressed the needs and ways of the truly "private" economic activity. Where it does not abolish them, as it already has abolished free contracting in the labor market, it attains the same end by shifting the relative importance of existing legal forms—the legal forms pertaining to corporate business for instance as against those pertaining to the partnership or individual firm—or by changing their contents or meanings. The capitalist process, by substituting a mere parcel of shares for the walls of and the machines in a factory, takes the life out of the idea of property. It loosens the grip that once was so strong—the grip in the sense of the legal right and the actual ability to do as one pleases with one's own; the grip also in the sense that the holder of the title loses the will to fight, economically, physically, politically, for "his" factory and his control over it, to die if necessary on its steps. And this evaporation of what we may term the material substance of property—its visible and touchable reality—affects not only the attitude of holders but also that of the workmen and of the public in general. Dematerialized, defunctionalized and absentee ownership does not impress and call forth moral allegiance as the vital form of property did. Eventually there will be *nobody* left who really cares to stand for it—nobody within and nobody without the precincts of the big concerns.

IX

GROWING HOSTILITY

I. The Social Atmosphere of Capitalism

FROM the analysis of the two preceding chapters, it should not be difficult to understand how the capitalist process produced that atmosphere of almost universal hostility to its own social order to which I have referred at the threshold of this part. The phenomenon is so striking and both the Marxian and the popular explanations are so inadequate that it is desirable to develop the theory of it a little further.

1. The capitalist process, so we have seen, eventually decreases the importance of the function by which the capitalist class lives. We have also seen that it tends to wear away protective strata, to break down its own defenses, to disperse the garrisons of its entrenchments. And we have finally seen that capitalism creates a critical frame of mind which, after having destroyed the moral authority of so many other institutions, in the end turns against its own; the bourgeois finds to his amazement that the rationalist attitude does not stop at the credentials of kings and popes but goes on to attack private property and the whole scheme of bourgeois values.

The bourgeois fortress thus becomes politically defenseless. Defenseless fortresses invite aggression especially if there is rich booty in them. Aggressors will work themselves up into a state of rationalizing hostility[1]—aggressors always do. No doubt it is possible, for a time, to buy them off. But this last resource fails as soon as they discover that they can have all. In part, this explains what we are out to explain. So far as it goes—it does not go the whole way of course—this element of our theory is verified by the high correlation that exists historically between bourgeois defenselessness and hostility to the capitalist order: there was very little hostility on principle as long as the bourgeois position was safe, although there was then much more reason for it; it spread *pari passu* with the crumbling of the protecting walls.

2. But, so it might well be asked—in fact, so it is being asked in naïve bewilderment by many an industrialist who honestly feels he

---

[1] It is hoped that no confusion will arise from my using the verb "to rationalize" in two different meanings. An industrial plant is being "rationalized" when its productive efficiency per unit of expenditure is being increased. We "rationalize" an action of ours when we supply ourselves and others with reasons for it that satisfy our standard of values regardless of what our true impulses may be.

is doing his duty by all classes of society—why should the capitalist order need any protection by extra-capitalist powers or extra-rational loyalties? Can it not come out of the trial with flying colors? Does not our own previous argument sufficiently show that it has plenty of utilitarian credentials to present? Cannot a perfectly good case be made out for it? And those industrialists will assuredly not fail to point out that a sensible workman, in weighing the pro's and con's of his contract with, say, one of the big steel or automobile concerns, might well come to the conclusion that, everything considered, he is not doing so badly and that the advantages of this bargain are not all on one side. Yes—certainly, only all that is quite irrelevant.

For, first, it is an error to believe that political attack arises primarily from grievance and that it can be turned by justification. Political criticism cannot be met effectively by rational argument. From the fact that the criticism of the capitalist order proceeds from a critical attitude of mind, i.e., from an attitude which spurns allegiance to extra-rational values, it does not follow that rational refutation will be accepted. Such refutation may tear the rational garb of attack but can never reach the extra-rational driving power that always lurks behind it. Capitalist rationality does not do away with sub- or super-rational impulses. It merely makes them get out of hand by removing the restraint of sacred or semi-sacred tradition. In a civilization that lacks the means and even the will to discipline and to guide them, they will revolt. And once they revolt it matters little that, in a rationalist culture, their manifestations will in general be rationalized somehow. Just as the call for utilitarian credentials has never been addressed to kings, lords and popes in a judicial frame of mind that would accept the possibility of a satisfactory answer, so capitalism stands its trial before judges who have the sentence of death in their pockets. They are going to pass it, whatever the defense they may hear; the only success victorious defense can possibly produce is a change in the indictment. Utilitarian reason is in any case weak as a prime mover of group action. In no case is it a match for the extra-rational determinants of conduct.

Second, the success of the indictment becomes quite understandable as soon as we realize what acceptance of the case for capitalism would imply. That case, were it even much stronger than it actually is, could never be made simple. People at large would have to be possessed of an insight and a power of analysis which are altogether beyond them. Why, practically every nonsense that has ever been said about capitalism has been championed by some professed economist. But even if this is disregarded, rational recognition of the economic performance of capitalism and of the hopes it holds out for the future would require an almost impossible moral feat by the have-not. That performance stands out only if we take a long-run view; any pro-capitalist argument must rest on long-run considerations. In the short run, it is profits and inefficiencies that dominate the picture. In order to accept his lot, the leveler or the chartist of old would have had to comfort himself with hopes for his great-grandchildren. In order to identify himself with the capitalist system, the unemployed of today would have completely to forget his personal fate and the politician of today his personal ambition. The long-run interests of society are so entirely lodged with the upper strata of bourgeois society that it is perfectly natural for people to look upon them as the interests of that class only. For the masses, it is the short-run view that counts. Like Louis XV, they feel *après nous le déluge*, and from the standpoint of individualist utilitarianism they are of course being perfectly rational if they feel like that.

Third, there are the daily troubles and expectations of trouble everyone has to struggle with in any social system—the frictions and disappointments, the greater and smaller unpleasant events that hurt, annoy and thwart. I suppose that every one of us is more or less in the habit of attributing them wholly to that part of reality which lies without his skin, and *emotional* attachment to the social order—i.e., the very thing capitalism is constitutionally unable to produce—is necessary in order to overcome the hostile impulse by which we react to them. If there is no emotional attachment, then that impulse has its way and grows into a permanent constituent of our psychic setup.

Fourth, the ever-rising standards of life and particularly the leisure that modern capitalism provides for the fully employed workman . . . well, there is no need for me to finish the sentence or to elaborate one of the tritest, oldest and most stodgy of all arguments which unfortunately is but too true. Secular improvement that is taken for granted and coupled with individual insecurity that is acutely resented is of course the best recipe for breeding social unrest.

II. The Sociology of the Intellectual

Nevertheless, neither the opportunity of attack nor real or fancied grievances are in themselves sufficient to produce, however strongly they may favor, the emergence of active hostility against a social order. For such an atmosphere to develop it is necessary that there be groups to whose interest it is to work up and organize resentment, to nurse it, to voice it and to lead it. As will be shown in Part IV, the mass of people never develops definite opinions on its own initiative. Still less is it able to articulate them and to turn them into consistent attitudes and actions. All it can do is to follow or refuse to follow such group leadership as may offer itself. Until we have discovered social groups that will qualify for that role our theory of the atmosphere of hostility to capitalism is incomplete.

Broadly speaking, conditions favorable to general hostility to a social system or specific attack upon it will in any case tend to call forth groups that will exploit them. But in the case of capitalist society there is a further fact to be noted: unlike any other type of society, capitalism inevitably and by virtue of the very logic of its civilization creates, educates and subsidizes a vested interest in social unrest.[2] Explanation of this phenomenon, which is as curious as it is important, follows from our argument in Chapter VII, but may be made more telling by an excursion into the Sociology of the Intellectual.

1. This type is not easy to define. The difficulty is in fact symptomatic of the character of the species. Intellectuals are not a social class in the sense in which peasants or industrial laborers constitute social classes; they hail from all the corners of the social world, and a great part of their activities consist in fighting each other and in forming the spearheads of class interests not their own. Yet they develop group attitudes and group interests sufficiently strong to make large numbers of them behave in the way that is usually associated with the concept of social classes. Again, they cannot be simply defined as the sum total of all the people who have had a higher education; that would obliterate the most important features of the type. Yet anyone who had—and, save exceptional cases, nobody who had not—is a potential intellectual; and the fact that their minds are all similarly furnished facilitates understanding between them and constitutes a bond. Nor would it serve our purpose to make the concept coextensive with the membership of the liberal professions; physicians or lawyers for instance are not intellectuals in the relevant sense unless they talk or write about subjects outside of their professional competence which no doubt they often do—particularly the lawyers. Yet there is a close connection between the intellectuals and the professions. For *some* professions—especially if we count in journalism—actually do belong almost wholly to the domain of the intellectual type; the members of *all* professions have the opportunity of becoming intellectuals; and many intellectuals take to some profession for a living. Finally, a definition by means of the contrast to manual labor would be much too wide.[3] Yet the Duke of Wellington's "scribbling set" seems to be too narrow.[4] So is the meaning of *hommes de lettres*.

[2] Every social system is sensitive to revolt and in every social system stirring up revolt is a business that pays in case of success and hence always attracts both brain and brawn. It did in feudal times—very much so. But warrior nobles who revolted against their superiors attacked individual persons or positions. They did not attack the feudal system as such. And feudal society as a whole displayed no tendencies to encourage—intentionally or unintentionally—attacks upon its own social system as a whole.

[3] To my sorrow, I have found that the Oxford English Dictionary does not list the meaning I wish to attach to the term. It does give the turn of phrase "a dinner of intellectuals," but in connection with "superior powers of intellect" which points in a very different direction. I have been duly disconcerted, yet have not been able to discover another term that would serve my purpose equally well.

[4] The Duke's phrase occurs in *The Croker Papers* (ed. L. J. Jennings, 1884).

But we might do worse than take our lead from the Iron Duke.
Intellectuals are in fact people who wield the power of the spoken
and the written word, and one of the touches that distinguish them
from other people who do the same is the absence of direct responsibility for practical affairs. This touch in general accounts for another—the absence of that first-hand knowledge of them which only
actual experience can give. The critical attitude, arising no less from
the intellectual's situation as an onlooker—in most cases also as an
outsider—than from the fact that his main chance of asserting himself
lies in his actual or potential nuisance value, should add a third touch.
The profession of the unprofessional? Professional dilettantism? The
people who talk about everything because they understand nothing?
Bernard Shaw's journalist in *The Doctor's Dilemma?* No, no. I have
not said that and I do not mean that. That sort of thing would be
still more untrue than it would be offensive. Let us give up trying
to define by words and instead define "epideiktically": in the Greek
museum we can see the object, nicely labeled. The sophists, philoso-
phers and rhetors—however strongly they objected to being thrown together, they were all of the same genus—of the fifth and fourth centuries B.C. illustrate ideally what I mean. That practically all of them
were teachers does not destroy the value of the illustration.

2. When analyzing the rationalist nature of capitalist civilization
(Chapter VII) I pointed out that the development of rational thought
of course precedes the rise of the capitalist order by thousands of
years; all that capitalism did was to give a new impulse and a particular bend to the process. Similarly—leaving aside the Graeco-Roman
world—we find intellectuals in thoroughly pre-capitalist conditions,
for instance in the Kingdom of the Franks and in the countries into
which it dissolved. But they were few in number; they were clergy-
men, mostly monks; and their written performance was accessible to
only an infinitesimal part of the population. No doubt strong individuals were occasionally able to develop unorthodox views and even
to convey them to popular audiences. This however in general implied
antagonizing a very strictly organized environment—from which at
the same time it was difficult to get away—and risking the lot of the
heretic. Even so it was hardly possible without the support or conniv-
ance of some great lord or chieftain, as the tactics of missionaries suffice to show. On the whole, therefore, intellectuals were well in hand,
and kicking over the traces was no joke, even in times of exceptional
disorganization and license, such as during the Black Death (in and
after 1348).

But if the monastery gave birth to the intellectual of the medieval
world, it was capitalism that let him loose and presented him with
the printing press. The slow evolution of the lay intellectual was
merely an aspect of this process; the coincidence of the emergence of

humanism with the emergence of capitalism is very striking. The humanists were primarily philologists but—excellently illustrating a point made above—they quickly expanded into the fields of manners, politics, religion and philosophy. This was not alone due to the contents of the classic works which they interpreted along with their grammar—from the criticism of a text to the criticism of a society, the way is shorter than it seems. Nevertheless, the typical intellectual did not relish the idea of the stake which still awaited the heretic. As a rule, honors and comfort suited him a great deal better. And these were after all to be had only from princes, temporal or spiritual, though the humanists were the first intellectuals to have a public in the modern sense. The critical attitude grew stronger every day. But *social* criticism—beyond what was implied in certain attacks on the Catholic Church and in particular its head—did not flourish under such conditions.

Honors and emoluments can however be had in more than one way. Flattery and subservience are often less remunerative than are their opposites. This discovery was not made by the Aretino[5] but no mortal ever surpassed him in exploiting it. Charles V was a devoted husband but, during his campaigns which kept him from home for many months at a time, he lived the life of a gentleman of his time and class. Very well, the public—and what particularly mattered to Charles, his empress—need never know, provided arguments of the right kind and weight were duly handed to the great critic of politics and morals. Charles paid up. But the point is that this was not simple blackmail which in general benefits one party only and inflicts uncompensated loss on the other. Charles knew why he paid though doubtless it would have been possible to secure silence by cheaper if more drastic methods. He did not display resentment. On the contrary he even went out of his way to honor the man. Obviously he wanted more than silence and, as a matter of fact, he received full value for his gifts.

3. In a sense, therefore, the Aretino's pen was indeed stronger than the sword. But, perhaps through ignorance, I do not know of comparable instances of that type for the next hundred and fifty years,[6] during which intellectuals do not seem to have played any great role outside and independently of the established professions, mainly the law and the church. Now this setback roughly coincides with the setback in capitalist evolution which in most countries of continental Europe occurred in that troubled period. And the subsequent recovery of capitalist enterprise was similarly shared by the intellectuals. The cheaper book, the cheap newspaper or pamphlet, together with the

[5] Pietro Aretino, 1492-1556.
[6] In England, however, the scope and importance of pamphleteering increased greatly in the seventeenth century.

widening of the public that was in part their product but partly an independent phenomenon due to the access of wealth and weight which came to the industrial bourgeoisie and to the incident increase in the political importance of an anonymous public opinion—all these boons, as well as increasing freedom from restraint, are by-products of the capitalist engine.

In the first three-quarters of the eighteenth century the individual patron was slow to lose the paramount importance in the intellectual's career that he had held at the beginning. But in the peak successes at least, we clearly discern the growing importance of the new element—the support of the collective patron, the bourgeois public. In this as in every other respect, Voltaire affords an invaluable instance. His very superficiality that made it possible for him to cover everything from religion to Newtonian optics, allied to indomitable vitality and an insatiable curiosity, a perfect absence of inhibitions, an unerring instinct for and a wholesale acceptance of the humors of his time, enabled that uncritical critic and mediocre poet and historian to fascinate—and to sell. He also speculated, cheated, accepted gifts and appointments, but there was always the independence founded on the solid base of his success with the public. Rousseau's case and type, though entirely different, would be still more instructive to discuss.

In the last decades of the eighteenth century a striking episode displayed the nature of the power of a free-lance intellectual who has nothing to work with but the socio-psychological mechanism called Public Opinion. This happened in England, the country that was then farthest advanced on the road of capitalist evolution. John Wilkes' attacks on the political system of England, it is true, were launched under uniquely favorable circumstances; moreover, it cannot be said that he actually upset the Earl of Bute's government which never had any chance and was bound to fall for a dozen other reasons; but Wilkes' *North Briton* was nevertheless the last straw that broke . . . Lord Bute's political back. No. 45 of the *North Briton* was the first discharge in a campaign that secured the abolition of general warrants and made a great stride toward the freedom of the press and of elections. This does not amount to making history or to creating the conditions for a change in social institutions, but it does amount to playing, say, the role of a midwife's assistant.[7] The inability of Wilkes' enemies to thwart him is the most significant fact

---

[7] I do not fear that any historian of politics will find that I have exaggerated the importance of Wilkes' success. But I do fear objection to my calling him a free lance and to the implication that he owed everything to the collective, and nothing to any individual patron. In his beginnings he was no doubt encouraged by a *coterie*. On examination it will however be conceded, I think, that this was not of decisive importance and that all the support and all the money and honors he got afterwards were but a consequence of and tribute to previous success and to a position independently acquired with the public.

about it all. They evidently had all the power of organized government at their command. Yet something drove them back.

In France, the years preceding the revolution and the revolution itself brought the rabble-raising tabloid (Marat, Desmoulins), which however did not, like ours, completely jettison style and grammar. But we must hurry on. The Terror and, more systematically, the First Empire put an end to this. Then followed a period, interrupted by the rule of the *roi bourgeois,* of more or less resolute repression that lasted until the Second Empire felt compelled to loosen the reins— about the middle sixties. In central and southern Europe this period also lasted about as long, and in England analogous conditions prevailed from the beginning of the revolutionary wars to Canning's accession to power.

4. How impossible it is to stem the tide within the framework of capitalist society is shown by the failure of the attempts—some of them prolonged and determined—made during that period by practically all European governments to bring the intellectuals to heel Their histories were nothing but so many different versions of Wilkes exploits. In capitalist society—or in a society that contains a capitalist element of decisive importance—any attack on the intellectuals must run up against the private fortresses of bourgeois business which, or some of which, will shelter the quarry. Moreover such an attack must proceed according to bourgeois principles of legislative and administrative practice which no doubt may be stretched and bent but will checkmate prosecution beyond a certain point. Lawless violence the bourgeois stratum may accept or even applaud when thoroughly roused or frightened, but only temporarily. In a purely bourgeois regime like that of Louis Philippe, troops may fire on strikers, but the police cannot round up intellectuals or must release them forthwith; otherwise the bourgeois stratum, however strongly disapproving some of their doings, will rally behind them because the freedom it disapproves cannot be crushed without also crushing the freedom it approves.

Observe that I am not crediting the bourgeoisie with an unrealistic dose of generosity or idealism. Nor am I unduly stressing what people think and feel and want—on the importance of which I almost, though not quite, agree with Marx. In defending the intellectuals as a group —not of course every individual—the bourgeoisie defends itself and its scheme of life. Only a government of non-bourgeois nature and non-bourgeois creed—under modern circumstances only a socialist or fascist one—is strong enough to discipline them. In order to do that it would have to change typically bourgeois institutions and drastically reduce the individual freedom of *all* strata of the nation. And such a government is not likely—it would not even be able—to stop short of private enterprise.

From this follows both the unwillingness and the inability of the capitalist order to control its intellectual sector effectively. The unwillingness in question is unwillingness to use methods consistently that are uncongenial to the mentality shaped by the capitalist process; the inability is the inability to do so within the frame of institutions shaped by the capitalist process and without submitting to non-bourgeois rule. Thus, on the one hand, freedom of public discussion involving freedom to nibble at the foundations of capitalist society is inevitable in the long run. On the other hand, the intellectual group cannot help nibbling, because it lives on criticism and its whole position depends on criticism that stings; and criticism of persons and of current events will, in a situation in which nothing is sacrosanct, fatally issue in criticism of classes and institutions.

5. A few strokes will complete the modern picture. There are the increasing means. There is the increase in the standard of life and in the leisure of the masses that changed and is still changing the composition of the collective patron for the tastes of whom the intellectuals have to provide. There was and is the further cheapening of the book and newspaper and the large-scale newspaper concern.[8] There is now the radio. And there was and is the tendency toward complete removal of restraints, steadily breaking down those short-run attempts at resistance by which bourgeois society proves itself so incompetent and occasionally so childish a disciplinarian.

---

[8] The emergence and the career up to date of the large-scale newspaper concern illustrate two points which I am anxious to stress: the manifold aspects, relations and effects of *every* concrete element of the social pattern that preclude simple and one-way propositions, and the importance of distinguishing short-run and long-run phenomena for which different, sometimes opposite, propositions hold true. The *large*-scale newspaper concern is in most cases simply a capitalist business enterprise. This does not *imply* that it espouses capitalist or any other class interests. It *may* do so, but only from one or more of the following motives, the limited importance of which is obvious: because it is subsidized by a capitalist group for the very purpose of advocating its interests or views—the larger the concern and its sales, the less important this element; because it intends to sell to a public of bourgeois tastes—this, very important until about 1914, now increasingly cuts the other way; because advertisers prefer to use a congenial medium—but mostly they take a very businesslike view of the matter; because the owners insist on a certain course irrespective of their interest in sales—to a certain extent, they do and especially did, but experience teaches that they do not hold out if the conflict with their pecuniary interest in sales is too severe. In other words, the large-scale newspaper concern is a most powerful tool for raising the position and increasing the influence of the intellectual group, but it is even now not completely in its control. It means employment and a wider public, but it also means "strings." These are mainly of importance in the short run; in fighting for greater freedom to do as he pleases, the individual journalist may easily meet defeat. But this short-run aspect—and the group's recollection of past conditions—are what enters the intellectual's mind and what determines the colors of the picture of slavery and martyrdom he draws for the public. In reality, it should be a picture of conquest. Conquest and victory are in this, as in so many other cases, a mosaic composed of defeats.

There is, however, another factor. One of the most important features of the later stages of capitalist civilization is the vigorous expansion of the educational apparatus and particularly of the facilities for higher education. This development was and is no less inevitable than the development of the largest-scale industrial unit,[9] but, unlike the latter, it has been and is being fostered by public opinion and public authority so as to go much further than it would have done under its own steam. Whatever we may think of this from other standpoints and whatever the precise causation, there are several consequences that bear upon the size and attitude of the intellectual group.

First, inasmuch as higher education thus increases the supply of services in professional, quasi-professional and in the end all "white-collar" lines beyond the point determined by cost-return considerations, it may create a particularly important case of sectional unemployment.

Second, along with or in place of such unemployment, it creates unsatisfactory conditions of employment—employment in substandard work or at wages below those of the better-paid manual workers.

Third, it may create unemployability of a particularly disconcerting type. The man who has gone through a college or university easily becomes psychically unemployable in manual occupations without necessarily acquiring employability in, say, professional work. His failure to do so may be due either to lack of natural ability—perfectly compatible with passing academic tests—or to inadequate teaching; and both cases will, absolutely and relatively, occur more frequently as ever larger numbers are drafted into higher education and as the required amount of teaching increases irrespective of how many teachers and scholars nature chooses to turn out. The results of neglecting this and of acting on the theory that schools, colleges and universities are just a matter of money, are too obvious to insist upon. Cases in which among a dozen applicants for a job, all formally qualified, there is not one who can fill it satisfactorily, are known to everyone who has anything to do with appointments—to everyone, that is, who is himself qualified to judge.

[9] At present this development is viewed by most people from the standpoint of the ideal of making educational facilities of any type available to all who can be induced to use them. This ideal is so strongly held that any doubts about it are almost universally considered to be nothing short of indecent, a situation not improved by the comments, all too often flippant, of dissentients. Actually, we brush here against a set of extremely complex problems of the sociology of education and educational ideals which we cannot attack within the limits of this sketch. This is why I have confined the above paragraph to two incontestable and noncommittal trivialities that are all we want for the purpose in hand. But of course they do not dispose of the larger problems which must be left aside to testify to the incompleteness of my exposition.

All those who are unemployed or unsatisfactorily employed or unemployable drift into the vocations in which standards are least definite or in which aptitudes and acquirements of a different order count.
They swell the host of intellectuals in the strict sense of the term
whose numbers hence increase disproportionately. They enter it in a
thoroughly discontented frame of mind. Discontent breeds resentment.
And it often rationalizes itself into that social criticism which as we
have seen before is in any case the intellectual spectator's typical attitude toward men, classes and institutions especially in a rationalist
and utilitarian civilization. Well, here we have numbers; a well-defined
group situation of proletarian hue; and a group interest shaping a
group attitude that will much more realistically account for hostility
to the capitalist order than could the theory—itself a rationalization
in the psychological sense—according to which the intellectual's right-
eous indignation about the wrongs of capitalism simply represents the
logical inference from outrageous facts and which is no better than
the theory of lovers that their feelings represent nothing but the
logical inference from the virtues of the beloved.[10] Moreover our
theory also accounts for the fact that this hostility increases, instead of
diminishing, with every achievement of capitalist evolution.

Of course, the hostility of the intellectual group—amounting to
moral disapproval of the capitalist order—is one thing, and the general hostile atmosphere which surrounds the capitalist engine is another thing. The latter is the really significant phenomenon; and it is
not simply the product of the former but flows partly from independent sources, some of which have been mentioned before; so far
as it does, it is raw material for the intellectual group to work on.
There are give-and-take relations between the two which it would
require more space to unravel than I can spare. The general contours
of such an analysis are however sufficiently obvious and I think it safe
to repeat that the role of the intellectual group consists primarily in
stimulating, energizing, verbalizing and organizing this material and
only secondarily in adding to it. Some particular aspects will illustrate the principle.

6. Capitalist evolution produces a labor movement which obviously
is not the creation of the intellectual group. But it is not surprising
that such an opportunity and the intellectual demiurge should find
each other. Labor never craved intellectual leadership but intellectuals
invaded labor politics. They had an important contribution to make:

[10] The reader will observe that any such theories would be unrealistic even if
the facts of capitalism or the virtues of the beloved were actually all that the social
critic or the lover believes them to be. It is also important to note that in the
overwhelming majority of cases both critics and lovers are obviously sincere; neither
psycho-sociological nor psycho-physical mechanisms enter as a rule into the lime-
light of the Ego, except in the mask of sublimations.

they verbalized the movement, supplied theories and slogans for it
—class war is an excellent example—made it conscious of itself and
in doing so changed its meaning. In solving this task from their own
standpoint, they naturally radicalized it, eventually imparting a revolutionary bias to the most bourgeois trade-union practices, a bias
most of the non-intellectual leaders at first greatly resented. But there
was another reason for this. Listening to the intellectual, the workman is almost invariably conscious of an impassable gulf if not of
downright distrust. In order to get hold of him and to compete with
non-intellectual leaders, the intellectual is driven to courses entirely
unnecessary for the latter who can afford to frown. Having no genuine
authority and feeling always in danger of being unceremoniously told
to mind his own business, he must flatter, promise and incite, nurse left
wings and scowling minorities, sponsor doubtful or submarginal cases,
appeal to fringe ends, profess himself ready to obey—in short, behave
toward the masses as his predecessors behaved first toward their ec-
clesiastical superiors, later toward princes and other individual patrons,
still later toward the collective master of bourgeois complexion.
Thus, though intellectuals have not created the labor movement, they
have yet worked it up into something that differs substantially from
what it would be without them.

   The social atmosphere, for the theory of which we have been gathering stones and mortar, explains why public policy grows more and
more hostile to capitalist interests, eventually so much so as to refuse
on principle to take account of the requirements of the capitalist
engine and to become a serious impediment to its functioning. The
intellectual group's activities have however a relation to anti-capitalist
policies that is more direct than what is implied in their share in verbalizing them. Intellectuals rarely enter professional politics and still
more rarely conquer responsible office. But they staff political bureaus,
write party pamphlets and speeches, act as secretaries and advisers,
make the individual politician's newspaper reputation which, though
it is not everything, few men can afford to neglect. In doing these
things they to some extent impress their mentality on almost everything that is being done.

   The actual influence exerted varies greatly with the state of the
political game from mere formulation to making a measure politically
possible or impossible. But there is always plenty of scope for it. When
we say that individual politicians and parties are exponents of class
interests we are at best emphasizing one-half of the truth. The other
half, just as important if not more so, comes into view when we consider that politics is a profession which evolves interests of its own—
interests that may clash with as well as conform to the interests of the

groups that a man or party "represents."[11] Individual and party opinion is, more than anything else, sensitive to those factors in the political situation that directly affect the career or the standing of the individual or party. Some of these are controlled by the intellectual group in much the same sense as is the moral code of an epoch that exalts the cause of some interests and puts the cause of others tacitly out of court.

Finally, that social atmosphere or code of values affects not only policies—the spirit of legislation—but also administrative practice. But again there is also a more direct relation between the intellectual group and bureaucracy. The bureaucracies of Europe are of pre- and extra-capitalist origin. However much they may have changed in composition as the centuries rolled on, they never identified themselves wholly with the bourgeoisie, its interests or its scheme of values, and never saw much more in it than an asset to be managed in the interest of the monarch or of the nation. Except for inhibitions due to professional training and experience, they are therefore open to conversion by the modern intellectual with whom, through a similar education, they have much in common,   while the tinge of gentility that in many cases used to raise a barrier has been fading away from the modern civil servant during the last decades. Moreover, in times of rapid expansion of the sphere of public administration, much of the additional personnel required has to be taken directly from the intellectual group—witness this country.

[11] This of course is just as true of the intellectuals themselves with respect to the class from which they come or to which, economically and culturally, they belong.

X

DECOMPOSITION

1. Faced by the increasing hostility of the environment and by the legislative, administrative and judicial practice born of that hostility, entrepreneurs and capitalists—in fact the whole stratum that accepts the bourgeois scheme of life—will eventually cease to function. Their standard aims are rapidly becoming unattainable, their efforts futile. The most glamorous of these bourgeois aims, the foundation of an industrial dynasty, has in most countries become unattainable already, and even more modest ones are so difficult to attain that they may cease to be thought worth the struggle as the permanence of these conditions is being increasingly realized.

Considering the role of bourgeois motivation in the explanation of the economic history of the last two or three centuries, its smothering by the unfavorable reactions of society or its weakening by disuse no doubt constitutes a factor adequate to explain a flop in the capitalist process—should we ever observe it as a permanent phenomenon—and one that is much more important than any of those that are presented by the Theory of Vanishing Investment Opportunity. It is hence interesting to observe that that motivation not only is threatened by forces external to the bourgeois mind but that it also tends to die out from internal causes. There is of course close interdependence between the two. But we cannot get at the true diagnosis unless we try to disentangle them.

One of those "internal causes" we have already met with. I have dubbed it Evaporation of the Substance of Property. We have seen that, normally, the modern businessman, whether entrepreneur or mere managing administrator, is of the executive type. From the logic of his position he acquires something of the psychology of the salaried employee working in a bureaucratic organization. Whether a stockholder or not, his will to fight and to hold on is not and cannot be what it was with the man who knew ownership and its responsibilities in the fullblooded sense of these words. His system of values and his conception of duty undergo a profound change. Mere stockholders of course have ceased to count at all—quite independently of the clipping of their share by a regulating and taxing state. Thus the modern corporation, although the product of the capitalist process, socializes the bourgeois mind; it relentlessly narrows the scope of capitalist motivation; not only that, it will eventually kill its roots.[1]

[1] Many people will deny this. This is due to the fact that they derive their impression from past history and from the slogans generated by past history during

2. Still more important however is another "internal cause," viz., the disintegration of the bourgeois family. The facts to which I am referring are too well known to need explicit statement. To men and women in modern capitalist societies, family life and parenthood mean less than they meant before and hence are less powerful molders of behavior; the rebellious son or daughter who professes contempt for "Victorian" standards is, however incorrectly, expressing an undeniable truth. The weight of these facts is not impaired by our inability to measure them statistically. The marriage rate proves nothing because the term Marriage covers as many sociological meanings as does the term Property, and the kind of alliance that used to be formed by the marriage contract may completely die out without any change in the legal construction or in the frequency of the contract. Nor is the divorce rate more significant. It does not matter how many marriages are dissolved by judicial decree—what matters is how many lack the content essential to the old pattern. If in our statistical age readers insist on a statistical measure, the proportion of marriages that produce no children or only one child, though still inadequate to quantify the phenomenon I mean, might come as near as we can hope to come to indicating its numerical importance. The phenomenon by now extends, more or less, to all classes. But it first appeared in the bourgeois (and intellectual) stratum and its symptomatic as well as causal value for our purposes lies entirely there. It is wholly attributable to the rationalization of everything in life, which we have seen is one of the effects of capitalist evolution. In fact, it is but one of the results of the spread of that rationalization to the sphere of private life. All the other factors which are usually adduced in explanation can be readily reduced to that one.

As soon as men and women learn the utilitarian lesson and refuse to take for granted the traditional arrangements that their social environment makes for them, as soon as they acquire the habit of weighing the individual advantages and disadvantages of any prospective course of action—or, as we might also put it, as soon as they introduce into their private life a sort of inarticulate system of cost accounting —they cannot fail to become aware of the heavy personal sacrifices that family ties and especially parenthood entail under modern conditions and of the fact that at the same time, excepting the cases of farmers and peasants, children cease to be economic assets. These sacrifices do not consist only of the items that come within the reach of the measuring rod of money but comprise in addition an indefinite

---

which the institutional change brought about by the big corporation had not yet asserted itself. Also they may think of the scope which corporate business used to give for illegal satisfactions of the capitalist motivation. But that would cut my way: the fact that personal gain beyond salary and bonus cannot, in corporate business, be reaped by executives except by illegal or semi-illegal practices shows precisely that the structural idea of the corporation is averse to it.

amount of loss of comfort, of freedom from care, and opportunity to enjoy alternatives of increasing attractiveness and variety—alternatives to be compared with joys of parenthood that are being subjected to a critical analysis of increasing severity. The implication of this is not weakened but strengthened by the fact that the balance sheet is likely to be incomplete, perhaps even fundamentally wrong. For the greatest of the assets, the contribution made by parenthood to physical and moral health—to "normality" as we might express it —particularly in the case of women, almost invariably escapes the rational searchlight of modern individuals who, in private as in public life, tend to focus attention on ascertainable details of immediate utilitarian relevance and to sneer at the idea of hidden necessities of human nature or of the social organism. The point I wish to convey is, I think, clear without further elaboration. It may be summed up in the question that is so clearly in many potential parents' minds: "Why should we stunt our ambitions and impoverish our lives in order to be insulted and looked down upon in our old age?"

While the capitalist process, by virtue of the psychic attitudes it creates, progressively dims the values of family life and removes the conscientious inhibitions that an old moral tradition would have put in the way toward a different scheme of life, it at the same time implements the new tastes. As regards childlessness, capitalist inventiveness produces contraceptive devices of ever-increasing efficiency that overcome the resistance which the strongest impulse of man would otherwise have put up. As regards the style of life, capitalist evolution decreases the desirability of, and provides alternatives to, the bourgeois family home. I have previously adverted to the Evaporation of Industrial Property; I have now to advert to the Evaporation of Consumers' Property.

Until the later decades of the nineteenth century, the town house and the country place were everywhere not only pleasant and convenient shells of private life on the higher levels of income, but they were indispensable. Not only hospitality on any scale and in any style, but even the comfort, dignity, repose and refinement of the family depended upon its having an adequate *foyer* of its own that was adequately staffed. The arrangements summarized by the term Home were accordingly accepted as a matter of course by the average man and woman of bourgeois standing, exactly as they looked upon marriage and children—the "founding of a family"—as a matter of course.

Now, on the one hand, the amenities of the bourgeois home are becoming less obvious than are its burdens. To the critical eye of a critical age it is likely to appear primarily as a source of trouble and expense which frequently fail to justify themselves. This would be so even independently of modern taxation and wages and of the attitude of modern household personnel, all of which are typical results of the capitalist process and of course greatly strengthen the case against what in the near future will be almost universally recognized as an outmoded and uneconomical way of life. In this respect as in others we are living in a transitional stage. The average family of bourgeois standing tends to reduce the difficulties of running the big house and the big country place by substituting for it small and mechanized establishments plus a maximum of outside service and outside life—hospitality in particular being increasingly shifted to the restaurant or club.

On the other hand, the home of the old type is no longer an indispensable requirement of comfortable and refined living in the bourgeois sphere. The apartment house and the apartment hotel represent a rationalized type of abode and another style of life which when fully developed will no doubt meet the new situation and provide all the essentials of comfort and refinement. To be sure, neither that style nor its shell are fully developed anywhere as yet and they proffer cost advantage only if we count in the trouble and annoyance incident to running a modern home. But other advantages they proffer already —the facility of using to the full the variety of modern enjoyments, of travel, of ready mobility, of shifting the load of the current little things of existence to the powerful shoulders of highly specialized organizations.

It is easy to see how this in turn bears, in the upper strata of capitalist society, upon the problems of the child. Again there is interaction: the passing of the spacious home—in which alone the rich life of a numerous family can unfold[2]—and the increasing friction with which it functions supply another motive for avoiding the cares of parenthood; but the decline of philoprogenitivity in turn renders the spacious home less worth while.

I have said that the new style of bourgeois life does not as yet offer any decisive cost advantage. But this refers only to the current or prime costs of servicing the wants of private life. As to overhead, even the purely pecuniary advantage is obvious already. And inasmuch as the outlay on the most durable elements of home life—especially the house, the pictures, the furniture—used to be financed mainly from previous earnings we may say that the need for accumulation of "consumers' capital" is drastically reduced by that process. This does not mean of course that demand for "consumers' capital" is at present, even relatively, smaller than it was; the increasing demand for durable consumers' goods from small and medium incomes more than counterbalances this effect. But it does mean that, so far as the hedonistic component in the pattern of acquisitive motives is concerned, the desirability of incomes beyond a certain level is reduced. In order to satisfy

[2] Modern relations between parents and children are of course partly conditioned by the crumbling of that steady frame of family life.

himself of this, the reader need only visualize the situation in a thoroughly practical spirit: the successful man or couple or the "society" man or couple who can pay for the best available accommodation in hotel, ship and train, and for the best available qualities of the objects of personal consumption and use—which qualities are increasingly being turned out by the conveyor of mass production[3]—will, things being what they are, as a rule have all they want with any intensity *for themselves*. And it is easy to see that a budget framed on those lines will be far below the requirements of a "seignioral" style of life.

3. In order to realize what all this means for the efficiency of the capitalist engine of production we need only recall that the family and the family home used to be the mainspring of the typically bourgeois kind of profit motive. Economists have not always given due weight to this fact. When we look more closely at their idea of the self-interest of entrepreneurs and capitalists we cannot fail to discover that the results it was supposed to produce are really not at all what one would expect from the rational self-interest of the detached individual or the childless couple who no longer look at the world through the windows of a family home. Consciously or unconsciously they analyzed the behavior of the man whose views and motives are shaped by such a home and who means to work and to save primarily for wife *and children*. As soon as these fade out from the moral vision of the businessman, we have a different kind of *homo oeconomicus* before us who cares for different things and acts in different ways. For him and from the standpoint of his individualistic utilitarianism, the behavior of that old type would in fact be completely irrational. He loses the only sort of romance and heroism that is left in the unromantic and unheroic civilization of capitalism—the heroism of *navigare necesse est, vivere non necesse est*.[4] And he loses the capitalist ethics that enjoins working for the future irrespective of whether or not one is going to harvest the crop oneself.

The last point may be put more tellingly. In the preceding chapter it was observed that the capitalist order entrusts the long-run interests of society to the upper strata of the bourgeoisie. They are really entrusted to the family motive operative in those strata. The bourgeoisie worked primarily in order to invest, and it was not so much a standard of consumption as a standard of accumulation that the bourgeoisie struggled for and tried to defend against governments that took the

---

[3] Effects on consumers' budgets of the increasing eligibility of mass-produced articles are enhanced by the price difference between them and the corresponding custom-made articles which increases owing to the increase in wages *pari passu* with the decrease in the relative desirability of the latter; the capitalist process democratizes consumption.

[4] "Seafaring is necessary, living is not necessary." Inscription on an old house in Bremen.

short-run view.[5] With the decline of the driving power supplied by the family motive, the businessman's time-horizon shrinks, roughly, to his life expectation. And he might now be--less willing than he was to fulfill that function of earning, saving and investing even if he saw no reason to fear that the results would but swell his tax bills. He drifts into an anti-saving frame of mind and accepts with an increasing readiness anti-saving *theories* that are indicative of a short-run *philosophy*.

But anti-saving theories are not all that he accepts. With a different attitude to the concern he works for and with a different scheme of private life he tends to acquire a different view of the values and standards of the capitalist order of things. Perhaps the most striking feature of the picture is the extent to which the bourgeoisie, besides educating its own enemies, allows itself in turn to be educated by them. It absorbs the slogans of current radicalism and seems quite willing to undergo a process of conversion to a creed hostile to its very existence. Haltingly and grudgingly it concedes in part the implications of that creed. This would be most astonishing and indeed very hard to explain were it not for the fact that the typical bourgeois is rapidly losing faith in his own creed. And this again becomes fully understandable as soon as we realize that the social conditions which account for its emergence are passing.

This is verified by the very characteristic manner in which particular capitalist interests and the bourgeoisie as a whole behave when facing direct attack. They talk and plead—or hire people to do it for them; they snatch at every chance of compromise; they are ever ready to give in; they never put up a fight under the flag of their own ideals and interests—in this country there was no real resistance anywhere against the imposition of crushing financial burdens during the last decade or against labor legislation incompatible with the effective management of industry. Now, as the reader will surely know by this time, I am far from overestimating the political power of either big business or the bourgeoisie in general. Moreover, I am prepared to make large allowances for cowardice. But still, means of defense were not entirely lacking as yet and history is full of examples of the success of small groups who, believing in their cause, were resolved to stand by their guns. The only explanation for the meekness we observe is that the bourgeois order no longer makes any sense to the bourgeoisie itself and that, when all is said and nothing is done, it does not really care.

Thus the same economic process that undermines the position of the bourgeoisie by decreasing the importance of the functions of entre-

[5] It has been said that in economic matters "the state can take the longer view." But excepting certain matters outside of party politics such as conservation of natural resources, it hardly ever does.

preneurs and capitalists, by breaking up protective strata and institutions, by creating an atmosphere of hostility, also decomposes the motor forces of capitalism from within. Nothing else shows so well that the capitalist order not only rests on props made of extra-capitalist material but also derives its energy from extra-capitalist patterns of behavior which at the same time it is bound to destroy.

We have rediscovered what from different standpoints and, so I believe, on inadequate grounds has often been discovered before: there is inherent in the capitalist system a tendency toward self-destruction which, in its earlier stages, may well assert itself in the form of a tendency toward retardation of progress.

I shall not stay to repeat how objective and subjective, economic and extra-economic factors, reinforcing each other in imposing accord, contribute to that result. Nor shall I stay to show what should be obvious and in subsequent chapters will become more obvious still, viz., that those factors make not only for the destruction of the capitalist but for the emergence of a socialist civilization. They all point in that direction. The capitalist process not only destroys its own institutional framework but it also creates the conditions for another. Destruction may not be the right word after all. Perhaps I should have spoken of transformation. The outcome of the process is not simply a void that could be filled by whatever might happen to turn up; things and souls are transformed in such a way as to become increasingly amenable to the socialist form of life. With every peg from under the capitalist structure vanishes an impossibility of the socialist plan. In both these respects Marx's *vision* was right. We can also agree with him in linking the particular social transformation that goes on under our eyes with an economic process as its prime mover. What our analysis, if correct, disproves is after all of secondary importance, however essential the role may be which it plays in the socialist credo. In the end there is not so much difference as one might think between saying that the decay of capitalism is due to its success and saying that it is due to its failure.

But our answer to the question that heads this part posits far more problems than it solves. In view of what is to follow in this book, the reader should bear in mind:

First, that so far we have not learned anything about the kind of socialism that may be looming in the future. For Marx and for most of his followers—and this was and is one of the most serious shortcomings of their doctrine—socialism meant just one definite thing. But the definiteness really goes no further than nationalization of industry would carry us and with this an indefinite variety of economic and cultural possibilities will be seen to be compatible.

Second, that similarly we know nothing as yet about the precise way by which socialism may be expected to come except that there must be a great many possibilities ranging from a gradual bureaucratization to the most picturesque revolution. Strictly speaking we do not even know whether socialism will actually come to stay. For to repeat: perceiving a tendency and visualizing the goal of it is one thing and predicting that this goal will actually be reached and that the resulting state of things will be workable, let alone permanent, is quite another thing. Before humanity chokes (or basks) in the dungeon (or paradise) of socialism it may well burn up in the horrors (or glories) of imperialist wars.[6]

Third, that the various components of the tendency we have been trying to describe, while everywhere discernible, have as yet nowhere fully revealed themselves. Things have gone to different lengths in different countries but in no country far enough to allow us to say with any confidence precisely how far they will go, or to assert that their "underlying trend" has grown too strong to be subject to anything more serious than temporary reverses. Industrial integration is far from being complete. Competition, actual and potential, is still a major factor in any business situation. Enterprise is still active, the leadership of the bourgeois group still the prime mover of the economic process. The middle class is still a political power. Bourgeois standards and bourgeois motivations though being increasingly impaired are still alive. Survival of traditions—and family ownership of controlling parcels of stock—still make many an executive behave as the owner-manager did of old. The bourgeois family has not yet died; in fact, it clings to life so tenaciously that no responsible politician has as yet dared to touch it by any method other than taxation. From the standpoint of immediate practice as well as for the purposes of short-run forecasting—and in these things, a century is a "short run"[7]—all this surface may be more important than the tendency toward another civilization that slowly works deep down below.

[6] Written in the summer of 1935.

[7] This is why the facts and arguments presented in this and the two preceding chapters do not invalidate my reasoning about the possible economic results of another fifty years of capitalist evolution. The thirties may well turn out to have been the last gasp of capitalism—the likelihood of this is of course greatly increased by the current war. But again they may not. In any case there are no *purely economic* reasons why capitalism should not have another successful run which is all I wished to establish.